PRAISE FOR *SPIRITUGRAPHICS*

"Knowing your customer is a fundamental truth for building a brand that lasts. Consumers have long been viewed through a demographic lens, but we know there's more to today's market. *Spiritugraphics* is the framework for any brand looking to engage their consumer in a meaningful way."

—DAVID GREEN,
Chairman and CEO of Hobby Lobby

"Today's brands depend on emerging data and insights. The spiritugraphics study offers marketers more than research—it provides a playbook and perspective for reaching a large addressable market. This book is a staple for any leader looking to drive long-term value and loyalty for their brands."

—JIM MOTOS,
Senior Vice President,
Consumer Brands Division at Rich's

"*Spiritugraphics* is driven by deep consumer research and 'in the trenches' experience with leading brands. It's an actionable framework for marketers who want to capture consumer hearts and minds across a large US market that's waiting to hear from them. I've spent 20+ years leading marketing teams and can tell you with certainty that there has never been a more critical time to cut through the clutter and drive more relevance and more impactful marketing. This is the book that needed to be written."

—TIM KOPP,
CEO of Terminus and former Brand Leader
at Coca-Cola, P&G, and Salesforce

"While demographics and psychographics are essential fare for most advertisers, no one brings greater experience to Spiritugraphics than Brad Benbow and Phil Daniels. Now they have graciously shared their expertise in a 'must-read' book for anyone desiring business growth driven by deeper, authentic connections between their brand and consumers. In *Spiritugraphics*, research and agency executives, business owners, ministry leaders, brand managers, and readers will find relevant consumer intelligence backed by refreshingly actionable research that reveals a large, untapped consumer segment hidden in plain sight."

—NATHAN ESTRUTH,
former Vice President, Procter & Gamble

Spiritugraphics®

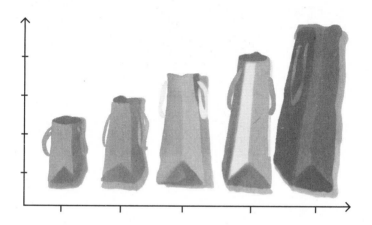

THE INFLUENCE OF FAITH
ON CONSUMPTION
AND WHY IT MATTERS
TO YOUR BRAND

BRAD BENBOW & PHIL DANIELS

Forefront
BOOKS

Published by Forefront Books.

ISBN: 978-1-63763-091-4 (Print)
ISBN: 978-1-63763-092-1 (eBook)

Library of Congress Control Number: 2022909302

Cover Design by Casey Harwood
Interior Design by Bill Kersey, KerseyGraphics

Over the past forty years I've enjoyed the loving support of a family like none other, putting up with the travel and late nights associated with the work we do. I dedicate my role in this book to my incredible wife and partner, Julie, my very best advisor and friend. We live a blessed life together.

As well, our three boys, Ty, Chance, and Bradley, grew up in this business and have learned to translate this experience into their roles in the world. My pride in them and my love for them is immeasurable.

I also dedicate this effort to the boys' wives, my daughters, Riley, Kyler, and Natalia. Incredible women who live out Spiritugraphics every day.

And finally, the little loves of my life, my grandkids, Berkeley, Decker, Zane, Bruno, Tucker, Fletcher, and Emilia. They are pure joy to me.

—Brad Benbow

To my mentors, advisors, clients, and business partners: You've taught me that influence is often disguised as impact. You've influenced me beyond measure and your impact is evident in this work—your love, guidance, and candor can't be overstated.

And to my family: You've endured the work-life integration that accompanies the chasing of dreams and big ideas. Lauren, you're the partner who makes life and everything in it better. Noah and Samuel, let's chase your dreams together.

—Phil Daniels

Contents

PART 1
What Is a Spiritugraphic?

PART 2
Ten Spiritugraphics

PART 3
Activating Spiritugraphics for Your Brand

PART 1

What Is a
Spiritugraphic?

CHAPTER 1

The Missing Data: Spiritugraphics

_____

*I ask you to forgive me for oversimplifying some
complicated subjects, and for the dogmatism of my
style—the dogmatism of brevity. We are both in a hurry.*
—DAVID OGILVY

What we do flows from who we are.
—CHUCK COLSON

What we believe determines how we behave. So much of what we think is good or right or beautiful is determined by what we believe. For those of us engaged in a life spent using various forms of communication to influence consumers to do things our clients want them to do, it is impossible to escape the dance of evaluating human behavior.

Why do we do the things we do? Why do we buy the things we buy? What causes us to take action? We all know these are complicated questions with far more complicated answers. Billions of dollars are spent each year trying to determine such answers and then cause engagement that leads to competitive advantage. Those of us who communicate for a living engage in attempts to influence what people within a given market think, believe, and do. Some of the smartest people I've ever met are the masters of this very thing. While medical- and tech-related trades are considered tougher, it is fair to argue that advertising and marketing are by far the most challenging of the occupations because we are dealing in entirely competitive environments, and there are no rules. This world is not for the timid.

What we believe determines how we behave.

A friend of mine, who is a very successful entrepreneur from Vancouver, talks about how the best marketers are inherently cowards. Obviously, marketing is a career that requires a great deal of courage and is subject to significant risk. Much of that risk is outside the control of even CMOs within most organizations. The accurate irony of my friend's comment is that great marketers leave as little to chance as possible. We are obsessive about data and information that provide insight into the actions and makeup of "users."

DATA, DATA, DATA

How old are they? What is their level of education? Where do they live? Do they have kids? Do they work? If so, what do they do? How much do they make? What is their ethnicity? How much time do they spend on social media? Who are their friends? What kind of car do they drive? Do they rent or own their house? Is that house in an inner-city location, in the suburbs, in a rural location, in a small town? What do the users read? What books, what magazines, what blogs? The list goes on and on and on. Why?

Because we all get paid to be right.

Clients and brands rely on their marketing teams and their advisors to provide insights and approaches that eventually cause revenue and market share gains. CEOs, and in particular CMOs, often see their own fortunes as leaders determined by such recommendations and the subsequent results. Anytime there appears to be missing data in the decision-making process, the efforts become far more high risk.

Is it possible that for decades brands have failed to make market share gains due to missing data about consumers?

Is it possible that for decades brands have failed to make market share gains due to missing data about consumers? It is not possible.

It is certain.

CULTURE AND BLIND SPOTS

Take any occupation or area of expertise, and eventually that consortium of individuals will refer to itself as a community. Like all communities, each will—over time—develop a culture that drives every form of thought and philosophy, manifesting into ideas we hear a lot about, including "best practices" or "social norms and values." Whether marketers or not, we all know we are products of our environment. As Peter Drucker famously said, "Culture eats strategy for lunch." Even those of us who consider ourselves strategists know that statement is true.

Culture drives everything. Culture also creates blind spots because we all know that we can't know what we don't know. However, just like we travel to new and interesting places, those of us from any culture venture into new lands occasionally. In the process, we discover new customs and new ideas.

As both a member of the world of communications—including marketing, advertising, and media—and a committed follower of Jesus, I've had the opportunity to see our community from a couple of vantage points. It dawned on me about a decade ago, after interactions with hundreds of clients and thousands of executives, that the worlds of faith and marketing are comprehensively detached from each other. And I couldn't help but ask myself why.

Perhaps because it's less common in the advertising and marketing industries to profess and practice faith in our work, it is impossible for the leaders in this space to ask questions about matters of faith. We can't know what we don't know. Most men and women in the marketing and advertising world identify with the position taken by *Mad Men*'s Don Draper: "I hate to break it to you, but there is no big lie, there is no system. *The universe is indifferent.*"[1]

Moreover, when someone from our community does have insight into those of faith, they characterize it within the concept of religion as opposed to faith. Here again, the blind spot causes problems. Contrary to popular belief, religion and faith are often not one and the same. So the question is compelling for all of us who consider ourselves market experts: *does faith influence consumption*?

THE PROXY FOR THE NOTION

It doesn't take long to see that this entire track is worth exploring. For the past sixty years, advertising and marketing have evaluated every imaginable attribute of the consumer. And yet there has been almost no consideration for the matters of faith in spite of obvious proxies for the notion. You will likely be surprised by how obvious this aspect of human behavior might be, given the active long-term examples that exist in the market. This book will explore the ways a consumer's faith influences their consumer habits. In the chapters that follow, we introduce ten primary categories where such habits are observed. These deeply rooted routines, which we will call *spiritugraphics,* include what we eat, how we dress, and how we view our existence. Consider for a moment how prevalent faith-based influences are within the US consumer market.

Illustrative example: The Jewish community by and large doesn't eat pork.

This is an example of spiritugraphics in play. While it is clearly a fact here in the US in 2022, it has also been historically true of the Jewish people across cultures for thousands of years. The heritage of the Jewish people has always considered pigs a "dirty" animal. Moreover, pigs are believed to harbor demons. Look no further than the fifth chapter of Mark's Gospel, which records Jesus sending a legion of demons into hundreds of pigs and then drowning them in the Sea of Galilee. Going further back in history, this behavior would have been dictated by the law of Moses. The point here? Jews don't eat pork.

And faith is the central reason.

Illustrative example: The Lenten tradition includes abstaining from meat.

This is perhaps the most obvious in the United States among proxies for the concept we call spiritugraphics. Lent is producing examples of faith influencing consumption every spring. Most US Catholics, who make up nearly 20 percent of the population, observe Lent. The primary thing Catholics give up during Lent is meat. This produces significant market effects each year as companies tout fish-based products.

Illlustrative example: Muslim men don't drink.

Making up less than 1 percent of the US market, Muslim men don't drink alcohol and don't wear gold jewelry because it's considered feminine. As you consider this for a moment, you'll realize these influences of faith have material bearing on how the jewelry sector would market to Muslim men, and how liquor advertisers might consider diversity representation in an accurate manner. When it comes to food, Muslims follow a similar kosher track, known as *halal*, as Jews do with the exception that Muslims also eat camel (a special provision directly from Muhammad). While there are only 3.5 million Muslims in America, one quarter of them have arrived since 2000, and that number is expected to increase to 8 million by 2050.[2]

Likewise, various denominations and movements of Christianity do not consume alcohol or tobacco of any kind.

Many have traditionally avoided activities including certain movies, card games, and various forms of gambling. This short list is a fairly broad range of consumption mentality entirely driven by perspectives derived from their faith.

HOW IS IT POSSIBLE WE'VE MISSED THIS?

Cultures adopt traditions and standards. Individuals develop what is known as a *worldview.* Simply put, how an individual sees the world, the lenses they look through, shapes the context of everything they consider. David Naugle, a leading expert on worldview, said:

> I submit that the most important issue in any person's life is not his or her education, career, finances, family or friendships. Rather, the most important issue in any person's life is that person's worldview because that person's worldview guides and directs everything else, including one's education, career, finances, family and friendships. [Worldview] is the basic cause, all else is effect or result.[3]

It is a profound notion. Think about how worldview shapes an individual's view of another individual. If your worldview sees humans as a highly evolved animal, an accidental happening, it can become easier to talk about people as "human capital" and "utility." If your worldview sees people as being created by a higher being, and placed here for special reasons and purposes, then they are likely to be viewed differently in terms of how they can be "used" and considered. This issue of origin is Exhibit A for the idea of worldview. But there are dozens, if not hundreds, of others. Francis Schaeffer, one

of the most prolific theologians of the twentieth century, said
the following about this topic:

> People have presuppositions . . . By "presupposi-
> tions" we mean the basic way that an individual
> looks at life—his worldview. The grid through
> which he sees the world. Presuppositions rest
> upon that which a person considers to be the truth
> of what exists. A person's presuppositions provide
> the basis for their values—and therefore the basis
> for their decisions.[4]

This is how a hunter can grab his shotgun and his bird
dog, take a walk in the woods, and consider it a spectacu-
larly beautiful scenario, while another person could see it
as immoral, dangerous, and inhumane. Same scene, two
worldviews.

So what does this have to do with spiritugraphics?
Few in the advertising, marketing, and media worlds have
a worldview activated by a practicing faith. Now, most
advertisers would tell you that this is exactly what they do
every day—see through a lens other than their own to sell
products and services to a population that is often very
different than themselves. And yet a significant percentage
of the population is being overlooked because few in the
advertising world see faith as informing consumption. This
work is an introduction to these lenses that both exist and
provide a line of sight into a substantially large component
of the overall US marketplace.

A READILY AVAILABLE AND
MATERIAL MARKET

As you read through the case for spiritugraphics, you'll see that the influences of faith are found around every corner and drive substantial consumption of everyday goods and services that make up our routine lives.

In chapter four we'll be reviewing the work of renowned behavioral researcher Britt Beemer. Mr. Beemer, who has advised and consulted some of America's most powerful business leaders, including Warren Buffett and Jack Welch, has executed over 1,800 national behavioral market studies over the past forty years. His theory related to market materiality is important to all of us who search for ways to give our clients a competitive edge. The conclusion is that any marketer who gains a 15 percent market awareness for a particular feature or benefit can shape the market to its image. This applies to product, pricing, and position.

In the pages that follow, you'll find many influences of faith that *surpass* such a threshold, and thus should be recognized in terms of their potential material impact when embraced and utilized for particular brands.

FAITH—MORE THAN A
PSYCHOLOGICAL CONDITION

Everyone in the worlds of advertising, marketing, and media is familiar with *geographics* (related to the structure of a particular region of land), *demographics* (related to the structure of a population of people), and *psychographics* (related to the structure of the human mind). As it pertains to the topic at hand, it might seem easy to take this subject matter and determine that it belongs in psychographics.

However, the difference between an opinion and a faith is significant. Opinions and trends can be fickle and malleable. On the other hand, matters of faith tend to be deep-seated. Psychology investigates the mind. Faith is a mechanism of the soul, and the soul is entirely different territory.

Faith is a mechanism of the soul, and the soul is entirely different territory.

Marketers are familiar with developing a tactic to locate a shared ethos between client and consumer. And yet when endeavoring to accomplish such a feat with a person of authentic faith, this venture takes on a new dimension. This new territory is the world of those who have the audacity to determine that their spiritual foundations dictate how they engage in commerce, and they represent more of the population—and the market—than we realize.

Keep in mind, the case being made for spiritugraphics intends to technically articulate the differences of these behavioral considerations, which, of course, clearly exist and are observable in our daily lives. Additionally, it might make initial sense for the marketing community to cram faith aspects into lifestyle analysis. While faith commitments sometimes manifest into lifestyle tendencies, they are not the same thing as lifestyle. Faith is far different and more influential. For example, money, income, or lack thereof causes changes in lifestyle. Faith is across all lifestyles while still influencing and informing lifestyle.

THE MISSING DATA: SPIRITUGRAPHICS

It is obvious that faith influences culture, societal beliefs, and, yes, the consumption of goods and services every day in America. But to what extent does faith influence our day-to-day purchasing decisions? We will explore great brands and marketers who answered this question long ago. We will also explore extraordinary case studies in which faith is the predominant factor in an otherwise secular proposition. We next take the time to review the landscape of the US market in terms of faith orientation, and the subsequent geographic and demographic makeups due to the influence of faith. Then we will have the opportunity to explore a new proprietary national behavioral study of adult women in America conducted by America's Research Group, which takes a deep dive into how women of faith live out their lives and buy based on those beliefs. Finally, we provide significant takeaways from these findings in tandem with recommendations toward activating initiatives based on these observations. It is our hope that what you derive from these pages will make a difference in how you maximize marketing your business or provide ever more precise advice as an influencer and/or expert. The missing data was never missing. It has been right in front of us.

CHAPTER 2

Forerunners and Benefactors

———

A really good creative person is more interested in earnestness than in glibness and takes more satisfaction out of converting people than in "wowing" them.
—LEO BURNETT

No account of the universe can be true unless that account leaves it possible for our thinking to be a real insight.
—C. S. LEWIS

Advertising is about taking insights and turning them into campaigns of conversion on behalf of products and services. Although David Ogilvy was correct in his estimation that ineffective ads can have a negative effect on product sales,[5] no one in the ad world willingly sets out to frustrate buyers away from a product or service. Nevertheless, it happens.

Perhaps this might be the greatest sense of hesitation toward spiritugraphics—the fear that delving into the relationship between faith and consumption could alienate too many consumers away from a product or service for the sake of a brief, marginal gain. Rest assured, we aren't suggesting you need to bring your client's products and services to church. However, opportunity exists to open up doors between your clientele and the consumers who practice their faith—without disenfranchising the rest of the consumer population. We know this to be true, because it has already happened.

Fortunately, several companies have already shown a propensity for threading the needle between appealing to consumers of faith and maintaining universal appeal.

These forerunners of spiritugraphics deserve to be highlighted, and we owe it to ourselves to study how they succeeded.

CHICK-FIL-A

The chicken sandwich war is in full swing with a seemingly endless list of challengers presenting their offerings to the hungry masses. Yet most consumers would admit the war was over before it began. For all the fast-food vendors who have trotted out a signature chicken sandwich, one has clearly dominated the market. And the quality of its sandwich is only part of the equation.

Chick-fil-A is not only the king of chicken sandwiches, it is one of the most prolific fast-food vendors in the nation. How has Chick-fil-A gone from a regional phenomenon into a national powerhouse?

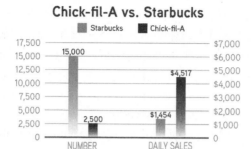

Chick-fil-A vs. Starbucks

There are approximately 2,500 Chick-fil-A stores (or units) nationwide. As of 2020, the average daily sales per unit at Chick-fil-A was $4,517, generating over $11 million per day in nationwide sales.[6] For context, Starbucks has over 15,000 units. A Starbucks unit averages $1,454 per unit per day, generating just over $21 million per day nationwide. In other words, Starbucks has six times as many units as Chick-fil-A, but does not even double it in overall sales. The average Chick-fil-A location is trouncing the local competition.

How does Chick-fil-A do against other fast-food titans? When one observes the unit-to-unit performance, Chick-fil-A remains the clear victor. Let's consider them for a moment compared to the three popular burger chains Burger King, McDonald's, and Wendy's.

	Units	Daily Sales per Unit	Daily Nationwide sales
Chick-fil-A	2,500	$4,517	$11,292,500
Burger King	7,346	$1,399	$10,300,000
McDonald's	13,846	$2,912	$40,413,000
Wendy's	5,852	$1,666	$9,865,000[7]

Chick-fil-A is an outright winner in overall sales versus Burger King and Wendy's despite having a significant disadvantage in the total number of units. Likewise, Chick-fil-A even substantially outduels McDonald's in unit-to-unit performance.

The same trends continue when Chick-fil-A goes toe-to-toe with its counterparts in the world of fried chicken. The average Zaxby's unit generates $2,030 per day in sales. Bojangles earns $1,717 per day, Popeye's $1,541, and KFC $1,196.[8]

Chick-fil-A is a powerhouse, the best pound-for-pound fast-food vendor in the country.

In his assessment of consumers choosing their favorite whiskey, David Ogilvy was correct when he said, "It isn't whiskey they choose, it's the image—*they are tasting images.*"[9] This logic certainly applies to other products, including chicken sandwiches. What is far more likely to be true than the argument that "Chick-fil-A has the most superior tasting sandwich" is that Chick-fil-A has built and maintained a national reputation along with a clear brand image. What is the essence of this reputation?

Perhaps the simplest way to summarize would be to say that Chick-fil-A has convinced the American population that they value people over the transaction, and they have amassed a fortune in the process: win-win!

The late Truett Cathy, founder of Chick-fil-A, cast the following vision for his growing brand: "We should be about more than selling chicken: we should be part of our customers' lives and the communities in which we serve."[10] Cathy was outspoken in running his business from a faith conviction, and he prioritized the notion that people need to have more than their bellies filled when they come in for a meal. This instinct has paid enormous dividends.

People of faith personally identify with the essence of the chain, becoming deeply loyal to the brand. And, of course, nobody hates being treated kindly; thus, a universal appeal has emerged. Such success was accomplished while also closing all stores on Sundays, operating from a standpoint of faith. This adds another impressive wrinkle to how Chick-fil-A measures up to its competition. The average Chick-fil-A manages to outperform other restaurants while working from a deficit on the number of days they are open to the consuming public.

However, it is the decision to *market* themselves as such that has led to such immense growth. It is one thing to develop an in-store experience. It is another thing entirely to make that experience the essence of the entire chain's relational marketing strategy.

What is far more likely to be true than the argument that "Chick-fil-A has the most superior tasting sandwich" is that Chick-fil-A has built and maintained a national reputation along with a clear brand image.

The sixth episode of *Mad Men*'s inaugural season, titled "Babylon," contains an iconic scene in which the creative team at Sterling Cooper is pitching Belle Jolie lipstick. The dialogue between Draper and the Belle Jolie executive serves as a telling metaphor for Chick-fil-A's relational marketing strategy.

At the time of Sterling Cooper's campaign pitch, Belle Jolie is the fourth-largest lipstick company in the country. The "Mark Your Man" sales pitch seeks to move Belle Jolie away from endless variety and into a more specific strategy. When the client expresses immediate skepticism, Don Draper's response becomes one of the more memorable moments in the series. He calls the client a nonbeliever! The climax of the intense conversation goes as follows:

Client: I don't think your three months and however many thousands of dollars allow you to refocus the core of our business.

Don Draper: Listen, I'm not here to tell you about Jesus. You already know about Jesus. Either he lives in your heart or he doesn't. Every woman wants choices. But in the end, none wants to be one of a hundred in a box.[11]

Draper believed Belle Jolie's performance was waning because women felt invisible in the seemingly endless variety of lipstick shades. They were a mere commodity among another ninety-nine commodities. The "Mark Your Man" campaign aspired to turn the locus of attention back on the woman buying the product. Draper's argument and the ideology of Chick-fil-A are aligned in this way. Chick-fil-A has insisted on seeing beyond a mere transaction, giving each patron a positive, relational—even personal—experience. Chick-fil-A has gone so far as to insist that this be the core of their marketing strategy. No one feels like one of a hundred in a box while they're eating at Chick-fil-A.

Skeptics might make the argument that positioning a chain as both faith-based and patron-centric lends oneself to public criticism that other chains don't have to worry about. Perhaps the most obvious example emerged when Truett Cathy made public comments in support of traditional marriage in 2012. This led to protests in various cities, threats to boycott the store, and efforts to remove locations on university campuses. Ironically enough, these efforts failed to gather momentum. It seems the protests weren't bad for business after all. A 2012 poll conducted by Rasmussen revealed that 63 percent of those polled held a favorable view of Chick-fil-A and only 13 percent would participate in a boycott.

It is one thing to develop an in-store experience. It is another thing entirely to make that experience the essence of the entire chain's relational marketing strategy.

And yet, despite the controversy over Chick-fil-A's traditional stance on marriage and the implications it has for the LGBTQ community, there is at least one occasion in which a Chick-fil-A restaurant has opened on a Sunday. This rare occurrence happened at two Orlando Chick-fil-A locations immediately following the Pulse nightclub shooting on Sunday, June 12, 2016. Pulse Nightclub, an LGBTQ bar, was intentionally targeted by a shooter aiming to commit an act of violent prejudice against such patrons. At the time, the Pulse Nightclub shooting was the deadliest mass shooting in American history, with forty-nine humans killed and more than fifty injured.

In the immediate aftermath of the shooting, at least two local Chick-fil-A stores were opened that Sunday by staff volunteers. The workers at these locations prepared food and delivered it to the victims and first responders of the horrific prejudicial attack, as well as those who were in line to donate blood. This case study reveals Chick-fil-A's ethos as a Christian vendor. Though the restaurant had previously come under fire for its position on marriage, Chick-fil-A acted from a place of compassion when an act of horrific prejudice was committed against people on the margins of society.

Chick-fil-A stands as exhibit A for the argument that there is a robust market for companies operating from an authentic Christian ethic.

IN-N-OUT BURGER

Such success in the food-service industry is not exclusive to the Atlanta-based chicken sandwich empire. The California-based burger joint In-N-Out Burger has been an innovative operation since the first location opened in 1948. Among its long list of accomplishments, In-N-Out Burger was the first restaurant in California to implement the drive-through. As well, it was In-N-Out Burger that first implemented the two-way speaker system that has become customary at virtually every drive-through restaurant.

The restaurant boasts a notable list of fans. Legendary chef Julia Child and world-traveling food critic Anthony Bourdain were both vocal fans. Kylie Jenner publicly craved In-N-Out Burger during one of her high-profile pregnancies, and the likes of Miley Cyrus, Reese Witherspoon, and

Brie Larson have all publicly shown off their In-N-Out grub while wearing award show glam.

And yet In-N-Out Burger also draws attention for what is featured on its packaging. If a patron pays close attention, they will discover a host of messages printed on the cups, wrappers, and boxes. What each of the messages have in common is that they are all Bible verses. For instance, on the inside lip of any soda cup, one will find John 3:16 written in little red letters. Likewise, burger wrappers reference Revelation 3:20, and French fry holders feature Proverbs 24:16—among several other verses.

The fact-finding website Snopes has perhaps the best commentary on this feature of the In-N-Out Burger experience: "These tiny notations are placed in out-of-the-way spots. No overt explanation is given for the presence of the odd phrases or their meaning: They just quietly sit there, awaiting decipherment by those moved to do so .... As proselytizing goes, this is about as lowkey as it gets."[12]

Much like the Cathys with Chick-fil-A, the California-based burger chain has been exclusively owned by one Christian family. At the writing of this book, the current sole owner of In-N-Out Burger is forty-year-old Lynsi Snyder, one of the youngest billionaires in the country and a devout Christian. Snyder has given credit for the Bible verses on the packaging to her late uncle, Richard Snyder. The restaurant began implementing Bible verses on packaging in 1987.[13]

Lynsi Snyder continues a long tradition of a vibrant in-house culture within In-N-Out that rivals that of Chick-fil-A. Snyder, who has been president of the company since age twenty-eight, was rated by Glassdoor as the number three CEO in America for 2019.[14] One reason why Snyder maintains such loyalty might be because In-N-Out Burger has long paid employees greater than federal minimum wage, and every employee earns a free meal each shift.

This commitment to maintaining high morale has been a priority since at least 1984 when In-N-Out University was founded. The training center, designed specifically for branch managers, focuses on food quality, cleanliness, and customer service, features that have become mainstays at each In-N-Out Burger location and have helped amass a major cult following.

Where the Georgia-based Chick-fil-A is outspoken about its Christian values deep in the Bible Belt, In-N-Out Burger has taken a more subtle, nuanced approach to incorporating its faith into its food service enterprise.

There is no doubt that In-N-Out Burger is a signature California food destination in its own right. Yet while the religious convictions of the Snyder family appear similar to that of the Cathy family, the manner in which their two restaurant chains leverage their faith is different. Where the Georgia-based Chick-fil-A is outspoken about its Christian values deep in the Bible Belt, In-N-Out Burger has taken a more subtle, nuanced approach to incorporating its faith into its food service enterprise.

In this way, the California-based burger chain has enjoyed near universal popularity. This is another example of threading the needle between opening the door to an entire segment of consumers and not jeopardizing one's overall appeal.

HOBBY LOBBY

Michael's and Hobby Lobby craft stores opened within one year of each other in neighboring states, the former opening in 1973 in Dallas and the latter in 1972 in Oklahoma City. Since that time, both companies have become retail giants in the arts-and-crafts industry. Both boast an annual revenue of more than 5 billion dollars. Both employ more than forty thousand people, and both have several hundred stores across the nation.

The presence of both retailers speaks to the prolific nature of homemaking in America, but more importantly there is a message here on the ability to carve out a consistent customer following in such a competitive space. In the case of Hobby Lobby, the strategy centered primarily on fiscal generosity; their profits, when put up against their competitors, show how prolific their model has proven to be.

Since the company was founded, Hobby Lobby has given away over half a billion dollars in earnings to various Christian charities.[15] This fiscal generosity also manifests itself in employee compensation. Hobby Lobby has classically paid its employees nearly double the minimum wage requirement with consistent increases in hourly pay. In 2012 a full-time Hobby Lobby employee's minimum hourly pay was $13 compared to the national rate of $7.25.[16] In 2014 Hobby Lobby raised its minimum wage requirement for full-time employees to $15 an hour while the national rate remained at $7.25 an hour.[17] By 2020 Hobby Lobby increased its starting wage to $17 an hour.[18] Beginning January 1, 2022, Hobby Lobby raised its minimum full-time hourly wage to $18.50.[19] As of this writing in late 2021, the federal minimum wage requirement remains $7.25 an hour, with outlier states such as California and New York moving from $14 to $15 an hour beginning January 1, 2022.[20] Hobby Lobby outpaces even the most progressive states with its generous compensation, and Hobby Lobby's founder, David Green, insists this generosity stems from a Christian ethic. "You can't have a belief system on Sunday and not live it the other six days."[21]

However, not everyone on the Hobby Lobby payroll has received a pay increase; founder and CEO David Green's 2021 annual salary is the same as what he made in 2001.[22] In fact, the Green family—who have been the sole owners of Hobby Lobby since its founding—have signed away future profits of Hobby Lobby (in the event the company is sold) to a protected trust, with 90 percent of the company's value being given away to charity.[23] David Green later reflected on this decision in greater detail: "But no one has the ability for a company that's worth billions of dollars to ever touch the company, because it's all real simple: God says He owns it, so now we're the stewards."[24]

Hobby Lobby predicted that a position of fiscal generosity would resonate with consumers, especially evangelical Christians among whom such generosity is common. In a highly competitive field, Hobby Lobby's instincts proved to be correct. Revenue between the two arts-and-crafts retailers is neck and neck, even though Hobby Lobby has approximately 250 fewer stores in North America and

Michael's is open one day more each week. (Like Chick-fil-A, Hobby Lobby also closes its doors each Sunday.) It would appear that Hobby Lobby has taken Leo Burnett's insights regarding marketing from earnestness and not found them to be lacking.

Another key aspect of differentiation between the two stores is the emphasis on religious décor and literature that can be spotted in Hobby Lobby locations nationwide. Many of the products appeal to evangelical consumers, yet this does not deter Hobby Lobby from competing with its largest competitor. If anything, by providing an outlet for such consumption, Hobby Lobby has increased its overall position in the industry.

Hobby Lobby predicted that a position of fiscal generosity would resonate with consumers, especially evangelical Christians among whom such generosity is common. In a highly competitive field, Hobby Lobby's instincts proved to be correct.

Similar to Chick-fil-A, Hobby Lobby has had its religious moti-vations questioned publicly. In 2014, the case of *Burwell v. Hobby Lobby* was heard before the United States Supreme Court, and the decision was handed down that private corporations are allowed exemption from federal regulation on the basis of religious objection. As it pertained to Hobby Lobby, this allowed the retailer to not provide health care that violated its religious position on the sanctity of human life.

This was a polarizing position for the retailer to publicly make, and one could have forecast this would negatively impact the growth of the company. On the contrary, Hobby Lobby has thrived in the aftermath of its involvement in the Supreme Court decision bearing its name.

Perhaps authenticity is a sought-after trait after all when selling a product or service. Regardless of one's position concerning Hobby Lobby's legal battle or corporate strategy, it cannot be said that Hobby Lobby has failed to commit itself to a singular, earnest approach to doing business.

This is not a manifesto on religion or reproductive rights. It is, however, a case study for the significance of spiritugraphics. The notion that a retail giant could be caught up in a Supreme Court case revolving around *religion* and it not hurt the company's bottom line communicates that we have underestimated the way a significant percentage of the American consumer thinks and spends. And their dollars spend the same as the next person's.

TOMS

Perhaps the best case study belongs to the shoemaker TOMS, which essentially set out to help consumers "mark the world."

Founded by Blake Mycoskie in 2006, TOMS started with a simple business plan. For every pair of TOMS purchased by a consumer, the company would donate a pair of shoes to a child in need. The 1:1 model became synonymous with the company.

In essence, TOMS built an entire business around the notion that consumers were willing to "mark the world" through their consumption habits. TOMS was operating from the assumption that people were not only willing but eager to make purchases that they felt made a positive difference in the world. Irene Anna Kim put it this way in her 2020 article for *Business Insider*: "Brands having a social mission might be commonplace today, but TOMS was the one that made it mainstream."[25]

What has since been coined "caring capitalism" or "embedded giving" began as an instinct that consumers cared more about the impact of their purchases than businesses had previously realized, especially when a company could trace the purchase to a positive outcome. In essence, it has become clear that being charitable can actually make a profit when executed correctly.

Between 2006 and 2013, TOMS generated $250 million dollars in sales and donated more than 10 million pairs of shoes across the globe. As of 2018 TOMS had given away over 70 million pairs of shoes worldwide. And at its zenith in 2014, TOMS was valued at $625 million.[26]

The success of TOMS can once again be attributed to a savvy ability to generate widespread appeal from a position of charity. It is true that TOMS's success cannot be separated from its association with Christian charity. Founder Blake Mycoskie himself has publicly expressed his Christian faith[27] and has referenced how his convictions influence the work of his company: "Beliefs in terms of my values and morals are very much a part of the center of TOMS."[28]

Yet it is undeniable that the appeal of TOMS transcended a single faith movement. This became clear when Mycoskie faced backlash for speaking at a Focus on the Family event in Orange County in 2011. Many who would reject an evangelical label voiced their confusion and frustration that TOMS's chief shoe giver would associate the TOMS brand with such an entity.[29]

It is rare in the polarizing world we live in today for a company to exist in which both evangelicals and progressives personally identify with a company's mission, yet this is exactly what TOMS achieved. So rampant was this success that the business model has since multiplied—even at expense to TOMS.

For instance, shoe company Skechers has since taken the iconic Alpargata slip-on shoe style from TOMS and designed its own. BOBS from Skechers sell for less than TOMS, and the shoe company pledges to donate two pairs of BOBS for every pair purchased. The embedded giving strategy has since expanded beyond footwear. Warby Parker has rolled out a similar strategy for eyewear; a strategy subsequently adopted by TOMS. IKEA has pledged that for every LED light bulb sold at an IKEA store worldwide, IKEA will donate one solar-powered desk lamp to a child living without electricity.[30]

Today examples of caring capitalism are so rampant that a reader is likely able to identify half a dozen more examples of embedded generosity in the corporate world. Clearly, Blake Mycoskie foresaw a burgeoning market that prior to then had been untapped. How deep this market goes and the effect it can have on the world remain to be discovered.

The argument for spiritugraphics made by Chick-fil-A, In-N-Out Burger, Hobby Lobby, TOMS, and the like is twofold: earnestness is profitable, and consumers are aware (at some level) of what their buying power can accomplish. For a significant percentage of the population, these features are founded on faith. When companies address this dynamic, it can lead to enormous profitability and increased market share.

And yet perhaps the best news of all is that one does not need to be a forerunner to spiritugraphics to benefit from it. The next best thing to being a spiritugraphics forerunner is to be a benefactor of it. A corporate altar call is not required—just an honest use of the data available.

> *Earnestness is profitable and consumers are aware (at some level) of what their buying power can accomplish.*

WENDY'S AND ARBY'S

The food industry has been monetizing Lent for several decades now. Virtually all fast-food companies market their fish sandwich between Ash Wednesday and Easter, regardless of whether they personally affiliate with any religion. The now iconic Filet-O-Fish sandwich at McDonald's was originally introduced during Lent in 1962.[31] It was so popular that it has become a stalwart on the McDonald's menu. However, two companies in particular have utilized Lent in a way that is strategic in comparison to other companies. Most fast-food vendors offer some form of fish sandwich all year and highlight it during Lent. This is not the case for Wendy's or Arby's.

Both of these restaurant chains have successfully carved out particular market strengths. Wendy's offers premium hamburgers and the best meal deal lineup in fast food. Arby's is notorious for roast beef and curly fries. Both of these companies have a very clear vision for who they are and where they are heading, and this includes a significant shift in focus each fiscal year.

Here is a little experiment: if you are reading this book after Easter and before Lent, log on to the Wendy's and Arby's websites and take a look at their menus. As of the third quarter of 2021, you will not find fish. Set a reminder on your phone for the week of Ash Wednesday and then return to their websites. On each menu an Alaskan pollock filet sandwich will have materialized.

By the end of spring, these sandwiches will have migrated off the menu.

These decisions by Wendy's and Arby's are driven solely by the behaviors of consumers of faith in America. Restaurants such as Wendy's and Arby's are widely known for offering niche items from which a notable percentage of the population consistently abstains at the same time every single year—roast beef in Arby's case and premium beef hamburgers in the case of Wendy's. Wendy's and Arby's, like most fast-food chains, are not affiliated with any one particular expression of faith, yet they actively adjust their menus to fit the religious expression of their customer base annually for a significant period of time. What is more, neither company will waste resources on keeping a fish sandwich on the menu year-round, because outside of Lent it is apparently not profitable for them to do so.

This is not a statement of faith by either restaurant. It is simply an example of companies enjoying a fiscal benefit from the utilization of spiritugraphics.

SEAPAK SHRIMP & SEAFOOD COMPANY

Founded in 1948, SeaPak Corporation began as a small but innovative frozen-food pioneer. SeaPak was acquired by Rich Products Corporation (Rich's) twenty-eight years later for just under $100,000.

Today SeaPak Shrimp & Seafood Company is the number one retail brand in the frozen specialty seafood category, a half-billion-dollar market leader. The prolific success of SeaPak can be attributed to the company's primary marketing strategy—to dominate and win Lent each year. Our agency, JDA Worldwide, has experienced this growth firsthand, having represented SeaPak for over fifteen years.

The prolific success of SeaPak can be attributed to the company's primary marketing strategy—to dominate and win Lent each year.

Up until the early 2000s, the major marketing and trade investment for the brand existed within the forty-six days between Ash Wednesday and Easter, primarily with in-store promotion and freestanding inserts. Year-over-year incremental growth led to national distribution of three product favorites: jumbo butterfly shrimp, popcorn shrimp, and shrimp scampi. By 2004 SeaPak premiered as one of the first brands to take over the Food Network's website on Ash Wednesday, kicking off a forty-day flight of national media placement and an upward journey as a category leading advertiser.

Culturally, Lent was not just the most important marketing and trade season for SeaPak. *Lent was the only season.* By 2014 the next milestone became expanding frequency of purchases inside the Lenten season, eventually creating a market beyond Lent. Summer and fourth-quarter holiday seasons have benefited most from this emphasis. The health benefits and special entertainment value shrimp offer have helped. Ultimately, however, the added revenue and resources gained by winning Lent each year have been the driving force in SeaPak's ascent.

> *Culturally, Lent was not just the most important marketing and trade season for SeaPak.* Lent was the only season.

A FINAL CASE STUDY—CHRISTMAS RETAIL

What is the largest card-sending holiday of the year? One might think it is Valentine's Day or perhaps even Mother's Day. Which holiday accounts for the most flower sales? Once again, one might suspect holidays geared toward romance or our mothers. Perhaps it might come as a surprise to discover that Christmas far surpasses any other holiday for greeting card and flower sales. Thirty percent of all flower sales are accounted for during Christmas and Hanukkah.[32] As well, Christmas accounts for 1.6 billion greeting cards sold, with the runner-up Valentine's Day accounting for 151 million cards sold.[33]

These are only a pair of examples for how the Christmas season serves as the primary driver of commerce annually. No other period in our culture leads to more economic impact than the days leading up to Christmas.

Why?

Because regardless of one's religious affiliation, the retail world orbits around the arrival of Jesus every year. To be fair, such consumer behavior has much more in common with Ricky Bobby leading his dysfunctional family in a prayer to "baby Jesus" than it does devout religious practice. Nevertheless, commerce is measured based off activity leading up to December 25.

> *Even the most agnostic retailer would begrudgingly admit that if it wants to be most profitable, Advent is the best time of year to drive profits.*

No company with an aim to turn a significant profit would ever ignore the deluge of capital that spills into stores nationwide during Advent. And at the risk of sounding redundant, this is not an expression of religious conviction; it is an effective utilization of spiritugraphics. Even the most agnostic retailer would begrudgingly admit that if it wants to be most profitable, Advent is the best time of year to drive profits. These are true insights, and this is the time for businesses to win converts.

In the chapters ahead, we will build a profile of who these customers are and what they care about.

CHAPTER 3

Americans and Faith

———

*You don't stand a tinker's chance of producing
successful advertising unless you start by doing
your homework. I have always found this extremely
tedious, but there is no substitute for it.*
—DAVID OGILVY

*If men do indeed have . . . real aspirations for
personal fulfillment in a universe that is finally
impersonal, then those aspirations are ultimately
unfulfillable and finally meaningless.*
—FRANCIS SCHAEFFER

In line with Francis Schaeffer's reflection, there is a
notable percentage of the American population who
will always refuse the notion of a universe void of ultimate
meaning. That our existence is random and the product
of mere chance is a view that a sizable population of the
American public rejects outright. This belief influences

how such members of the populace choose services and consume products. Such consumers not only exist but make up a significant portion of the American population. So who are they? Better yet, where are they?

Thus far we have introduced you to this missing piece of data in the world of advertising and taken a peek behind the curtain at various companies that have utilized this knowledge for corporate growth. Now we will endeavor to create a basic portrait of who these consumers are, along with the scope of their collective presence in the market.

Starting in 1850 the United States Census tracked religious affiliation among Americans. Citing concerns regarding the separation of church and state, this practice was discontinued in 1950. In the wake of this decision, various entities have maintained a robust study of religious affiliation across the American landscape.

American Religion

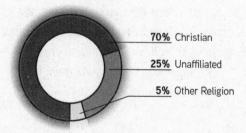

70% Christian

25% Unaffiliated

5% Other Religion

The 2020 Census of American Religion conducted by Public Religion Research Institute (PRRI) determined that 70 percent of Americans identify as Christian.[34] One quarter of the American population identified as unaffiliated, and another 5 percent specified another religion.

The extent of America's Christian identity transcends ethnicity, age, politics, education, and gender. In other words, a business or vendor cannot identify a Christian consumer based off any data one might usually employ to identify a particular consumer base. Christian faith in America is not confined to rurality or urbanity, gender, ethnicity, economic nor education status. In chapters 4 and 5 we will draw distinctions between specific Christian consumers, but as it pertains to Christianity's representation nationwide there is no prototypical Christian.

ETHNICITY

Christian Ethnicity

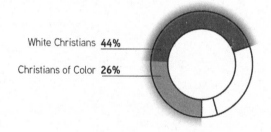

White Christians **44%**

Christians of Color **26%**

PRRI's 2020 American Religious Landscape Study revealed that 44 percent of Americans identify as a White Christian and are well represented across evangelicalism, mainline Protestantism, and Catholicism.[35] Over a quarter of Americans (26 percent) identify as Christians of color. Hispanics skew more toward Catholicism, but Black Protestants significantly outnumber Black Catholics. In total, 71 percent of White Americans, 72 percent of Black Americans, 76 percent of Hispanic Americans, and

55 percent of multiracial Americans identify with the Christian faith.

Percent Christian by Ethnicity

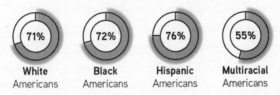

71%	72%	76%	55%
White	**Black**	**Hispanic**	**Multiracial**
Americans	Americans	Americans	Americans

AGE

Every age bracket of American adult is represented by a Christian majority. Americans aged 18–29 are the least likely to identify as Christian (54 percent), but the proclivity to identify as such rises steadily with each subsequent generation.[36]

This steady increase in religious belief across generations is actually expected. In 2008 the American Religious Identification Survey (ARIS) coined the term "Nones" to describe the seemingly ominous growth of young Americans choosing not to identify with a religion.[37] Since that time, the overall percentage of Americans who identify as religiously unaffiliated has decreased, with rates among Americans aged 18–29 and 30–49 falling respectively.[38]

In fact, Pew Research Center's 2014 Religious Landscape Study revealed that 33 percent of all American Christians were between the ages of 30 and 49. This was a larger percentage than ages 50–64 (29 percent) or 65-plus (21 percent).[39]

In other words, American adults tend to steadily align more with the Christian faith as they exit early adulthood, either because they have returned to a faith heritage or are new Christians.

POLITICS

Not even politics frustrates American religious identification. Both Republicans (83 percent) and Democrats (69 percent) identify as Christian.[40] However, White American Christians and American Christians of color do deviate in their loyalty between the two parties. More than two-thirds of Republicans (68 percent) identify as White Christian, while only 8 percent of Republicans identify as Christians of color. Meanwhile, American Democrats are 38 percent White Christian and 27 percent Christians of color.[41]

EDUCATION

Americans identifying as Christian possess dominant representation across all education levels. For instance, the largest portion of the American population to possess a high school education or less are Hispanic Catholics (65 percent).[42] Likewise, White evangelical Protestants (30 percent) and White mainline Protestants (30 percent) are most likely to possess some college experience.[43] Finally, White Catholics (27 percent) are tied with members of the Jewish faith for the largest segment of the American population to possess a college degree.[44]

GENDER

Gender representation has proven consistent in the twenty-first century for American Christians, with women representing 54 percent of the American Christian population in 2008[45] and 55 percent in 2014.[46] In fact, there is not a single American Christian denomination in which the male population exceeds the female population. The largest disparity is found in the Pentecostal tradition, which skews 58 percent toward women.

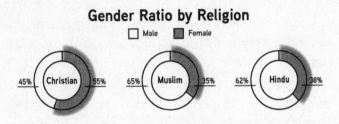

Gender Ratio by Religion

This is a fascinating insight because such a breakdown is not the case in the populations of other religions. Muslim men (65 percent) outpopulate women (35 percent) at a similar rate that Hindu men (62 percent) outpopulate women (38 percent).[47]

This is especially important as it pertains to our current topic for it is predominantly women who drive commerce. A 2019 *Forbes* study revealed that American women drive 70–80 percent of all consumer purchasing decisions.[48] Women even account for over 50 percent of purchases of traditional male products.[49] In 2019 American women accounted for 6.4 trillion dollars of purchases.[50] Indeed, the American woman's perspective is critical to enjoying increases in the market.

WHERE IS THE AMERICAN CHRISTIAN HOUSEHOLD?

As we enter the third decade of the twenty-first century, it might come as a surprise that religious representation remains so high and so pervasive. As well as remaining spiritually committed, Americans maintain key theological beliefs tethered to faith. For instance, when Pew Research Group conducted a religious landscape study of America, it found that 83 percent of all Americans believed in God—63 percent were absolutely certain while another 20 percent were fairly certain.[51] The same study revealed that 98 percent of evangelical Protestants, 98 percent of historically Black Protestants, 91 percent of mainline Protestants, and 91 percent of Catholics believe in God.[52]

The Pew Religious Landscape study also found that 87 percent of Americans believe religion is important to one's life.[53] Once again, evangelical Protestants (96 percent) and historically Black Protestants (97 percent) led the way on these beliefs with Catholics (90 percent) and mainline Protestants (87 percent) not far behind.[54] Finally, a majority of Americans believe in heaven (70 percent) and hell (58 percent).[55]

A 2019 Forbes study revealed that American women drive 70–80 percent of all consumer purchasing decisions.

However, the 2020 PRRI study revealed different sects of Christian faith appear to vary regionally. White evangelical Protestants are heavily concentrated in the South–Southeast of the country. For instance, there are eighty-one American counties across eleven states with a White evangelical population of 60 percent or higher, all of which can be found no farther north than Kentucky and no farther west than Oklahoma.[56] American counties with a White evangelical population of 50 percent or

higher crawl as far west as Colorado, stretching north-
ward into pockets of Nebraska, Kansas, Iowa, Illinois, and
Indiana.[57] Twenty-two American counties are at least 50
percent Black Protestant and can be found only from
Louisiana to South Carolina.[58]

For context, there is not a single American county
consisting of a mainline Protestant or Catholic population
higher than 45 percent.[59] Slope County, North Dakota, has
eight hundred residents, with mainline Protestants making
up 44 percent of the population.[60] Forty-five percent of
Dubuque County, Iowa's, 97,000 residents identify as
Catholic.[61] Lackawanna County, Pennsylvania's, population
of 210,000 is also 45 percent Catholic.[62] Hispanic Catholics
making up 50 percent of the population of American counties are found exclusively in Texas, Arizona, and Southern
California.[63]

Such widespread regional intensity is not sustained
across other faiths. Rockland County, New York's, 18
percent Jewish population is the largest of its kind.[64]
Middlesex County, New Jersey, is 7 percent Hindu.[65] As
well, the Muslim population makes up 5 percent of Queen's
County, New York—the largest of its kind.[66] Hawaii County,
Hawaii's, 5 percent Buddhist population is also the largest
for this faith nationally.[67]

Perhaps most remarkably, there is not a single American
county in which half or more of the population is religiously
unaffiliated. San Juan County, Washington, and its population of eighteen thousand residents is 49 percent unaffiliated, the largest percentage in America.[68] Monroe County,
Indiana's, 41 percent unaffiliated population is the largest of
its kind between New York and the Mississippi River.[69]

America is a religious nation. Not only is the American population religious, but their religious background leads to unique consumer activity. Based only on the activity of consumers belonging to our clients at JDA Worldwide—for whom we have extensive data—we are able to ascertain that there are no fewer than 38 million Christian-centric consumer households.[70] Thirty-eight million.

This an enormous number of households. The question now is whether it is possible to build a profile for this segment of the American population. Our agency represents clients and brands in Christian entertainment, tourism, ministry, and charitable giving spaces. By studying which households spend and donate their money to such services and attractions, we unlock a fascinating portrait of how vast spiritugraphics is as a study.

Based only on the activity of consumers belonging to our clients at JDA Worldwide—for whom we have extensive data—we are able to ascertain that there are no fewer than 38 million Christian-centric consumer households.

The top Christian spenders subgroups in our in-house research tend to be situated in small-town and rural contexts. They are middle- to upper-middle-income young families who drive American-made automobiles, shop at sporting goods stores, go on vacation, eat at chain restaurants, and tune in for sporting events and DIY shows. And there are over 8 million households such as these.

Top Christian donor subgroups tend to be upper-class, middle-aged families and empty nesters who have accumulated significant wealth and are situated in the suburbs. Such households are more likely to follow and play golf and tennis, spend time at a country club, drive a high-end import, and take international vacations. Once again, there are another 8 million households fitting this unique description and remember, these are only the top households in each segment.

Christian households are active, engaged, and one would likely not even realize they were interacting with such a household.

Christian households are predominantly spread out across Middle America in rural, small-town, and suburban populations, with middle- to upper-scale incomes. Many are starting families or sending their children to college. Christian households are active, engaged, and one would likely not even realize they were interacting with such a household.

DISSATISFIED WITH THE INSTITUTION

Although faith is a significant marker of the American population, a 2020 Gallup study revealed that only 47 percent of Americans belong to a church, synagogue, or mosque.[71] There is currently a disconnect between religious identity and religious fraternity. Another Gallup study revealed American satisfaction with the influence of organized religion fell from 59 percent in 2020 to 48 percent in 2021.[72]

In the past two decades, the two largest-growing religious demographics are the unaffiliated and Christian (nonspecified).[73] The American Religious Identification Survey (ARIS) tracked religious views from 1990 to 2008. One of its primary findings took note of how American Christians prefer to describe and affiliate themselves. In 1990 fewer than 200,000 Americans preferred being called nondenominational.[74] By 2008 over 8 million Americans preferred the term.[75] The Gallup Historical Religious Preference Data charted the long-term religious views of Americans from 1948 to 2020. Prior to 2000 there was no data point for the nonspecified Christian. Less than two decades later, the Christian nonspecified designation accounted for 10 percent of those polled.[76]

Americans are frustrated with the institutional church. What this clearly illustrates is that Christianity in America is not only being challenged from the outside but, from within.

Such a shift in religious affiliation among American Christians is not centralized generationally either. When comparing church membership rates captured between 2008 and 2010 to rates captured between 2018 and 2020, one will find that membership has fallen across every generation, including Baby Boomers, Generation X, and Millennials.[77] Americans of all ages are struggling to identify with the institutions that have historically represented American Christianity. The same trends are true concerning gender, ethnicity, marital status, and political affiliation. Americans are frustrated with the institutional church. What this clearly illustrates is that Christianity in America is not only being challenged from the outside but, from within.

This is critical to our analysis today. Americans are still largely religious yet they are finding themselves less satisfied with the influence of their religious entities and less likely to attend a worship service. How, then, will an American of faith express their faith?

You guessed it—in the marketplace. Thus the struggles of the church are inevitably becoming the struggles of the business world. Virtually every formal institution is waking up to the reality that people no longer inherently trust or approve of the modus operandi, and this is true on both sides of the political aisle. For instance, only 26 percent of Americans—24 percent of Democrats and 31 percent of Republicans—approve of the size and influence of major corporations.[78] If the American Christian has ceased to identify with a religious institution at the same rate as was once historically the case, it is imperative for the advertiser to recognize the same phenomenon as it takes place in the marketplace.

If the American Christian has ceased to identify with a religious institution at the same rate as was once historically the case, it is imperative for the advertiser to recognize the same phenomenon as it takes place in the marketplace.

The marketplace will certainly reveal that Christian consumers will move away from the institutions that mirror the failings of their churches. In fact, this might already be happening more than the industry realizes. In 2014 Gabe Rosenberg reported that 91 percent of American women feel that advertisers don't understand them.[79] Since there are more American Christian women than men, women are the predominate spenders, and an overwhelming majority of women feel misunderstood by marketers, then there is a good bet we in advertising are leaving an extraordinary amount of money on the table.

How a business chooses to market itself to this large and frustrated percentage of the population will be critical in the years ahead. Crucial questions must be asked and answered: What frustrates this segment of the population? What inspires them? The correct answers to these questions could unlock exponential growth in revenue for your business or your client. Fortunately, exactly such a study has been conducted, and the incredible results can be found in the next chapter.

If there are more American Christian women than men, women are the predominate spenders, and an overwhelming majority of women feel misunderstood by marketers, then there is a good bet we in advertising are leaving an extraordinary amount of money on the table.

CHAPTER 4

America's Research Group National Behavioral Study

———

If you can't turn yourself into your customer, you probably shouldn't be in the ad-writing business at all.
—LEO BURNETT

Man stands at the juncture of nature and spirit; and is involved in both freedom and necessity.
—REINHOLD NIEBUHR

Consumers are driven toward material needs but they're also driven by a proclivity to consume beyond mere need. For some, this aspect of freedom embedded in consumption can become one's primary means of identity. This essence is what graphic designer Barbara Kruger sought to communicate in her 1990 image *I shop therefore I am*. Consumers today view themselves by what they purchase and consume. In Barbara's own words:

The existence of self becomes embedded with the act of consuming. In the analysis of the texts, I show that advertisements create self-doubts and guilt by comparing people in real life with the unattainable ideal people. This could potentially destroy the foundation of people's perception and security of self. The unbridgeable difference between "who I am" and "who I should be" propels people to engage in consumption.[80]

But this is surely not the case for all people. What is far more likely to be true today is that people do not purchase and consume to *find* an identity but rather to *reinforce* their identity in a particular group or tribe. The American Christian household is just such a population. In fact, born-again Christians make most of their decisions for their family based on faith. As we at JDA Worldwide represented clients and brands that target households of faith, we discovered the spiritugraphics framework. We commissioned America's Research Group to conduct a national behavioral study into this significant segment of the population. The results were fascinating and have major implications for the advertiser that desires to penetrate this consumer group.

A few key highlights from the previous chapter include that 70 percent of Americans believe in God and that there are at least 38 million Christian households. These two realities serve as the foundation for spiritugraphics, but the details are where the true insights lie.

METHODOLOGY

This qualified study, commissioned by JDA Worldwide and conducted by America's Research Group, consisted of a sample of 1,000 American women interviewed nation-wide over the phone by a random digit procedure. Such a method is important as it ensures the construction of a probability sample.

The first question that might arise is, Why women? As we established in the last chapter, women are the drivers of commerce in the American household, even as it concerns many men's products. As such, this makes women a great proxy for such a study since they are the buyers of most things in American culture. Another question one might ask is, How proportionate to region was this study? You may recall that religious devotion can be more heavily concen-trated in particular areas of the country. If a study were to emphasize one particular region over another, this could affect the quality of the results. Women interviewed for this study were represented across six regions:

- **New England/Mid-Atlantic**—Connecticut, Maine, Massachusetts, New Hampshire, New Jersey, New York, Pennsylvania, Rhode Island, and Vermont
- **South Atlantic**—Delaware, District of Columbia, Florida, Georgia, Maryland, North Carolina, South Carolina, Virginia, and West Virginia
- **East/North Central**—Illinois, Indiana, Michigan, Ohio, and Wisconsin
- **South Central**—Alabama, Arkansas, Kentucky, Louisiana, Mississippi, Oklahoma, Tennessee, and Texas

- **North Central Mountain**—Arizona, Colorado, Idaho, Iowa, Kansas, Minnesota, Missouri, Montana, Nebraska, Nevada, New Mexico, North Dakota, South Dakota, Utah, and Wyoming
- **Pacific**—Alaska, California, Hawaii, Oregon, and Washington

Of the 1,000 women interviewed, 179 lived in New England / Mid-Atlantic states (17.9 percent), 192 South Atlantic (19.2 percent), 154 East / North Central (15.4 percent), 177 South Central (17.7 percent), 138 North Central Mountain (13.8 percent), and 160 Pacific (16 percent).

In-store shopping is preferred by 54.7 percent, with 49.8 percent preferring to shop online. And yet only half find in-store shopping to be fun, and three in five said they could not recall the last time they experienced incredible customer service at a retail store.

Age was well represented across the spectrum as well. Women ages 34 or younger represented 16.4 percent of the study, ages 35–44 were 23.3 percent, ages 45–54 were 25 percent, ages 55–64 came in at 19 percent, and 65-plus was 16.3 percent.

Finally, over 65 percent possessed some college education and 70 percent were married and either actively raising children or empty nesters.

As for the nature of the interview, women were asked 133 questions over the phone. The questions predominantly analyzed the consumer habits of each

Respondent Demographics

1000 Women Surveyed

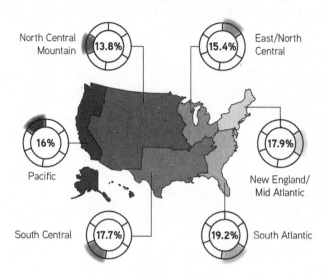

North Central Mountain **13.8%**

East/North Central **15.4%**

16% Pacific

17.9% New England/ Mid Atlantic

South Central **17.7%**

19.2% South Atlantic

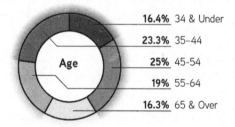

16.4% 34 & Under
23.3% 35–44
25% 45-54
19% 55-64
16.3% 65 & Over

Age

Education

65% Possessed some college education

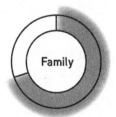

Family

70% Married with children or empty nesters

household, seeking to ascertain where they shop, what was important when shopping, were they shopping differently today, and did faith affect their shopping habits. Those interviewed were also asked questions pertaining to age, region, religion, media consumption, parental habits, and financial context.

The survey began December 11, 2020, and concluded January 27, 2021.

GENERAL FINDINGS

Americans appear united on a number of interesting topics.

Sensitivity concerning a family's kids appears to be nearly universal. Parental attention to their children's use of technology was particularly interesting. Seven out of ten women interviewed check the websites their children visit, and greater than three in five check the amount of time their children spend on a phone/tablet. As well, 82.5 percent believe social media has too much influence on teenagers today.

Survey questions that targeted how and where Americans shop reveal the ongoing battle between online and retail. In-store shopping is preferred by 54.7 percent, with 49.8 percent preferring to shop online. And yet only half find in-store shopping to be fun, and three in five said they could not recall the last time they experienced incredible customer service at a retail store.

Sixty-two percent indicated that they try to support local businesses, and 60 percent of respondents revealed that a store's reputation is at least somewhat important to them, with another 20 percent indicating it is very important.

Well over half of those surveyed indicated they had watched more television than they had been watching in the previous few months.

Do You Consider Yourself a Person of Faith?

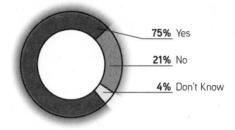

75% Yes

21% No

4% Don't Know

Some of the preliminary findings align heavily with religious data addressed in the previous chapter, but there is a further division that must be analyzed within spiritugraphics. While the overall American population is largely willing to embrace some semblance of faith identity, for many this appears to be merely window dressing. Their life is not affected by their faith in any tangible way. For example, of the 1,000 women interviewed, 75 percent believe God created the world, and three in four believe they are a person of faith. However, five out of nine said faith does not affect how they shop. Fifty-five percent reported their household either does not attend church or attends sporadically. And 57 percent specified they have not had a transformational experience in which they accepted Jesus into their heart—or what evangelicals commonly refer to as being "born-again" in reference to Jesus's words in the third chapter of John's gospel.

Did You Have a Transformational Experience by Accepting Christ?

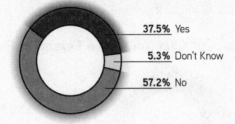

37.5% Yes

5.3% Don't Know

57.2% No

However, for those who acknowledged they have embraced this transformational experience—being born-again—there is a marked difference in their habits. Remember, this segment of Americans is no fewer than 38 million households. When we compare those who recognize this transformational experience, what differences in consumer habits emerge?

COMPARING THE "BORN-AGAINS" TO THE REST

We must not stop at the questions of whether consumers believe in God or considers themselves to be a person of faith. Both questions garnered 75 percent support in the study. The acknowledgment of a higher power does not alter behaviors such as church attendance or consumption. However, if an individual acknowledges a transformational spiritual experience, what is commonly referred to as being born-again— suddenly a significant shift occurs in behavior.

When we reexamine the data with emphasis on the disparity between those shoppers who indicated a transformational experience and those who did not, clear differences emerge. Respondents who had this transformational spiritual experience make up 37.5 percent of the qualified nationwide study. In other words, this segment is too big and too intentional in their behavior to be ignored. To do so would be to lose significant market share. So what are some of the differences in behavior between those who are born-again and those who have not indicated having had a transformational spiritual experience?

In-store shopping

Do You Prefer To Shop Online or In-Store?

☐ Online ◪ In-Store

32% | 68% — Transformed

53% | 47% — Not Transformed

In-store shopping is one such example. The gap widens significantly, as born-again shoppers prefer in-store to online shopping 68 percent to 32 percent. Those who did not indicate a transformational experience actually prefer online shopping 53.3 percent to 46.7 percent. Likewise, 60.8 percent of born-again shoppers find in-store shopping to be fun, whereas only 48.1 percent of those who did not indicate a transformational experience find it enjoyable. When asked if they want a salesperson available, shoppers who indicated a transformational

Born-again shoppers prefer in-store to online shopping 68 percent to 32 percent.

experience said *yes* 72.8 percent of the time; only 57.5 percent said *yes* among those who were not born-again.

This preference for in-store versus online shopping even appears to shape perception. When the survey asked respondents where they feel they will get the lowest price, those who indicated a transformational experience chose in-store 65.1 percent of the time compared to those who did not, who leaned toward online 55.1 percent of the time.

The reason why shopping is not fun also appears to differ between spiritugraphics. For instance, when asked why in-store shopping is not fun, born-again respondents cited concerns related to COVID-19 as the primary reason 47.4 percent of the time. Those who did not indicate a transformational experience cited COVID-19 concerns as the primary reason only 13.1 percent of the time. The leading culprit that makes shopping not fun for those without a transformational experience was lack of time at 20.7 percent.

Interactions with media

Significant shifts in how respondents interact with media were revealed across the spectrum of spiritugraphics. Concerns for the quality of the content varied drastically between those who indicated a transformational spiritual experience and those who did not. When asked if they would shop at a store that sold pornographic books or videos, 79.7 percent of those who indicated a transformational spiritual experience responded *no*, compared to 48.1 percent of those who did not indicate a transformational spiritual experience. Born-again respondents were 37.8 percent less likely to watch an R-rated movie compared to those who were not born-again. Likewise, born-again respondents were 34.8 percent less likely to know a family member who read Harry Potter. They were 27.6 percent less likely to have read *Fifty Shades of Grey*.

Relationship to money

One's relationship to money appears to vary significantly across spiritugraphic lines. These differences revealed themselves primarily in the arenas of credit cards, debt level, and generosity.

The most common number of credit cards per born-again household was *one* (39.5 percent) compared to *two* (37.2 percent) for non-born-again households. This might seem relatively miniscule, but when the results expand to include more of the respondent answers, the gap between the two spiritugraphics grows.

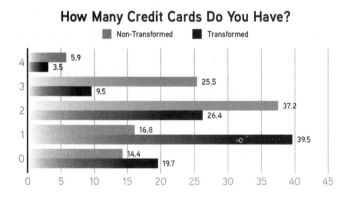

How Many Credit Cards Do You Have?

Respondents who did not report a transformational spiritual experience were more likely to own two, three, or four credit cards versus born-again respondents, who were more likely to own zero to one credit cards. Predictably, this proclivity to possess fewer credit cards leads to less pressure caused by debt. The survey asked recipients to describe the debt level of their family, with the options being that they felt no pressure, some pressure, or a lot of pressure. More than 50 percent of born-again households reported feeling no pressure caused by debt. Households that did not report a transformational spiritual experience were more likely to feel some or a lot of pressure caused by debt.

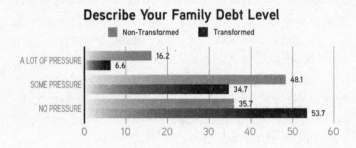

Describe Your Family Debt Level

It would make sense for one to observe the data and assume that the reason for such results lies in a disbalance pertaining to annual household income. Perhaps the discrepancy is tied to born-again households having a leg up financially on households that did not report a transformational spiritual experience.

In reality, there is no statistically significant difference in combined annual income between born-again households and their counterparts. If any discrepancy is to be made, it is that there are slightly more born-again households earning less than $35,000 annually and slightly more households not reporting a transformational spiritual experience earning $100,000–$149,999.

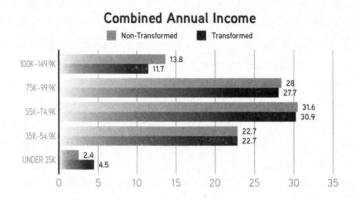

A clear discrepancy can also be observed in the area of charity. Households that reported a transformational spiritual experience reported being significantly more generous with their income. In fact, there are as many born-again households giving 9–10 percent of their annual income to charity (the typical tithe) as there are non-born-again households giving nothing to charity. Born-again households have higher representation in percentage of giving from 5 percent onward, with their counterparts better representing 0–4 percent giving.

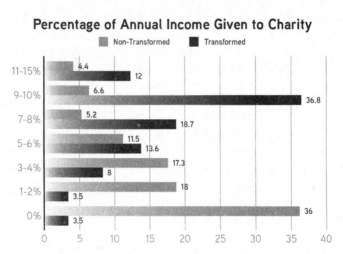

Supporting reputable companies

Predictably, born-again households were more likely to identify and value companies connected to Christian ethics. When respondents in the study were asked to identify a Christian-owned company, exactly 386 individuals could not name one. Exactly 386 other individuals mentioned Chick-fil-A. Another 159 respondents first mentioned Hobby Lobby.

When the survey asked respondents to mention a second Christian-owned company, 667 could not name one, 163 individuals identified Hobby Lobby, and another 97 mentioned Chick-fil-A.

Born-again households were more likely to identify and value companies connected to Christian ethics.

However, when the data is split between respondents who had a transformational spiritual experience and those who did not, the results come into clearer focus. The first-mentioned question about Christian-owned businesses saw 64 percent of born-again respondents name either Chick-fil-A or Hobby Lobby, with only 24.8 percent unable to mention a business. Only 50 percent of respondents who did not report a transformational spiritual experience named these two businesses, with 44.9 percent unable to name any such business.

These results intensified when the survey asked respondents to list another Christian-owned business. Forty-four percent of born-again respondents were unable to name a second business, compared to 79 percent of their counterparts in the study. More than 40 percent of born-again respondents named Chick-fil-A or Hobby Lobby as their second business, whereas fewer than 16 percent of the other respondents could do the same.

This awareness of Christian-owned business coupled with one's spiritual status led to interesting results. The survey asked respondents the compound question of whether they were aware of a Hobby Lobby store near them *and* whether they would shop at Hobby Lobby because it is a Christian-owned business. Respondents with no spiritually transformative experience were twice as likely to indicate that there was not a Hobby Lobby store near them compared to their born-again counterparts. In fact, only 10 percent of non-born-again respondents knew of a nearby Hobby Lobby and shopped there because it was Christian-owned. However, of these households that knew of a nearby Hobby Lobby, 57.5 percent indicated the retailer's Christian values did not influence their decision to shop there.

On the contrary, 37.6 percent of born-again respondents knew of a nearby Hobby Lobby and stated that they shopped at it because they knew it was a Christian-owned store, making them over 27 percent more likely to shop Hobby Lobby because of faith.

Such results were even more extreme regarding Chick-fil-A. Seventy percent of born-again households indicated that they ate at Chick-fil-A because of the chain's Christian values, whereas fewer than 33 percent of their counterparts indicated the same habit.

This type of loyalty, of course, ought to be expected. Respondents indicated as much during the study. When asked how faith has affected what they do or do not buy, a significant disparity emerged from the data.

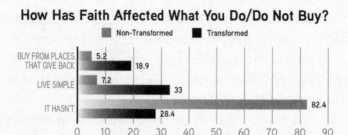

How Has Faith Affected What You Do/Do Not Buy?

Those in the study who considered themselves people of faith and also indicated a transformational spiritual experience were far more likely to indicate how faith influenced their consumption compared to their counterparts who described themselves as people of faith without a transformational experience. The latter indicated that faith had no such influence on their consumption.

This concept of faith determining consumption reveals itself in several different scenarios. Born-again respondents were 60 percent more likely to let their faith influence where they would go with their friends, 49 percent more likely to let their faith influence what movies they would see, and 50 percent more likely to let their faith influence the television programs they watch.

Family activities
The same trends apply to activities concerning their families. Born-again families were 45 percent more likely to let their faith influence what their children watched

and with which friends their children were allowed to go places. These same families were 46 percent more likely to allow their faith to influence the school activities in which their children could participate and 45 percent more likely to let their faith influence what they did together as a family.

Day Care
Finally, differences pertaining to day care are drastic. Between 55 and 60 percent of both groups indicated their children attended day care; however, the nature of the day care differed significantly.

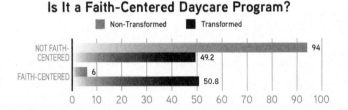

Is It a Faith-Centered Daycare Program?

When asked if the day care program was faith-centered, only 6 percent of families who did not indicate a transformational spiritual experience answered *yes*. When born-again respondents were asked the same question, just over half answered *yes*.

For a significant chunk of the population, faith is the driving factor of their decision-making; they make up far more of the population than most in our industry realize. The habits listed in the previous pages represent only the tip of the iceberg. The key aspects of differentiation await us in the next chapter—the ten spiritugraphics everyone needs to know.

This is where the rubber meets the road for this significant percentage of the market is engaged in commerce and
has spoken clearly about who they are and what they value.
Will those who are of persuasion in the industry speak to
them or will they miss them entirely? The answer to that
question will determine the flow of millions upon millions of
dollars toward or away from your clientele.

CHAPTER 5

Engaging a Large, Overlooked Market

———

We are mythic beings: we live by and in our symbols.
—LEANNE PAYNE, *HEALING PRESENCE*

Today's marketer relies on information. More than helpful inputs, data has become a staple in our work. Whether you're an emerging brand, category king, or advertising agency supporting client growth, information and insights are more than corporate lexicon—they inform our work. Consumer information underwrites how we identify, engage, and grow our given markets.

If we're crafting a brand, securing media time, or launching an app to court market share, our work is guided by long-standing sources of truth. Perhaps the most fundamental of these are the traditional demographics and psychographics discussed earlier. These two frameworks have trained us to know our audience—their traits, makeup, life experiences, and motivations all help paint a more complete picture of the consumer (and, ultimately, their motivations to take action).

Despite significant advances in technology and analytics, our industry's approach to consumer insights has remained relatively unchanged. In the pursuit of knowing the customer, brand leaders and agencies alike have exhausted demographics and psychographics. You've likely worked on campaigns that are governed by a creative brief that sounds something like, "Reaching a demo of 18–34, suburban, college-educated households with $75K+ income." Sound familiar?

Consumer information underwrites how we identify, engage, and grow our given markets.

These attributes are surely valuable but what if there's another dimension to understanding your consumer market— one that not only provides new insights but represents an even larger addressable market for your brand?

We realize any new marketing framework brings with it a multitude of questions and uncertainty—even if these later become an obvious set of insights. For example, before the adoption of demographics, was it obvious that the buying behaviors of men and women were different? Was it obvious that messages about the same product or concept would appeal to men or women in a more compelling fashion if they were crafted with the male or female audience in mind?

Further, was it obvious, before demographics, that the same distinctions would be true and highly valuable for businesses that tailored messages for different ages, economic levels, educational levels, and geographies?

And what about psychographics? Was it obvious that personalities would respond to the same offering if the marketer created targeted messaging for different personality types? Was it obvious that existing choices in lifestyles would be useful indicators of future buying behavior, and that studying the cross-reference was worth the marketer's time in addressing various market segments in nuanced ways? Was it obvious, before the development of psychographics, that interests, opinions, attitudes, and cultural perspectives would hold the keys for improved market penetration?

Today these are obvious and proven prescriptions for understanding your brand's market. More than just intuitively correct, the demographic and psychographic frameworks are the standard for segmenting and targeting our audiences. At their core, demographics and psychographics are a quest toward relevancy—the more tailored and relevant the message is to the consumer, the better.

At their core, demographics and psychographics are a quest toward relevancy—the more tailored and relevant the message is to the consumer, the better.

If we think of demographics as more or less the study of the physical self, the body, and if we think of psychographics as the mind and internal thought, what about the soul? How do we see and speak to that hidden, appetite-driven set of beliefs and affections in ways that illustrate value and drive action from those we serve or know as customers?

And where would a marketer even begin?

Broad buckets help illustrate general observations such as income and gender. Age ranges or dominant personality types, such as introversion versus extroversion, are critical for categorizing data and for making plans to act according to segments.

Then there's a "how much" dial that is also influenced by the relative strengths of other traits that impact how strong a particular consumer attribute might be. For example, when speaking to a "dominant male thinker," the dominant dial should be tuned differently than it would be to a "dominant male feeler," especially if one is a police officer in Detroit and the other is an elementary teacher in Colorado Springs.

To ensure our consumer intelligence is actionable, we need (1) external criteria, dropped into (2) a limited set of categories, with some way of seeing how (3) layers of insight impact the right answer to the question, "What's the best way to communicate to this person to influence behavior and consumption?"

INTRODUCING SPIRITUGRAPHICS: A FRAMEWORK FOR DEEPER CONSUMER ENGAGEMENT

The research in chapter four makes the case for spiritugraphics as an emerging framework to reach new audiences. It's a foray not into demographics of the body or psychographics of the mind, but into *spiritugraphics* of the soul.

Where demographics asks, "How can I expect behavior to vary according to various physical descriptions?" and where psychographics asks, "How can I expect behavior to vary according to various ways of thinking?" the study of spiritugraphics asks, "How can I expect behavior to vary according to the desires and spiritual experiences of the soul?"

In conducting a statistically valid study for this book, we started with the central question, "Does a consumer's faith influence their consumption?" *Our underlying objective of this work is to uncover the sizable market segment that is waiting for brands to find them.* Spiritugraphics benefits both marketers and consumers. We believe this because we've seen the market work for the good of both parties through the time-tested applications of demographics and psychographics. These two frameworks have contributed to more contextualized and relevant messaging for us as consumers. Yet as evidenced by our research of the born-again Christian segment, this third dimension, that of the consumer soul, can engage your audiences even more effectively (and personally). If you know more about who you're addressing and what moves them, you're more likely to address them in ways they'll find affirming, regardless of differences.

> *The study of spiritugraphics asks, "How can I expect behavior to vary according to the desires and spiritual experiences of the soul?"*

A QUICK REMINDER ABOUT OBJECTIVITY

As communication experts, we fully recognize the current era of charged emotions concerning all things tribal or traditional, and cultural discretion has taught us to steer clear of faith-forward topics that are explored in this book. But the purpose of our research is less theological and more capitalistic. Spiritugraphics is a framework to grow your reach, revenue, and market share, regardless of your beliefs and convictions. It's up to you how much you flex or incorporate these new learnings, and remember, it's not about what you personally believe.

We encourage you to remind yourself that studying the perspectives of religious people should be the same as studying the perspectives of women, blue-collar workers, rural communities, introverts, adventurers, and entrepreneurs. Marketers operate in a world of personas and matters of the heart within this audience are no exception. In every instance, gaining insights give you a choice to either engage with empathetic understanding to build a mutually rewarding relationship or to avoid targeting and communicating to a segment altogether. You don't have to become, or affirm the convictions of, the people whose purchasing power you seek. But as with any modern-day consumer, trust is earned when you show them you understand them.

NAVIGATING WITH SPIRITUGRAPHICS

In the previous chapters the pivotal realization pertaining to the spiritugraphics of the American consumer is that an undeniable disparity exists between those who nominally claim faith and those whose faith has entirely changed them so they now think and live differently. We call this transformational spiritual experience being born-again, and consumers are guided by what James Sire described as an absolute standard stemming from outside one's own conscience or judgments. As a result, this significant percentage of the American populace consumes in a considerably alternative fashion to other American consumers; they choose with much more discernment what they will and will not listen to from Madison Avenue.

This study of spiritugraphics reveals a large segment of the American population has been underserved. To be clear, this is not a new or emerging group. Its members have been in our midst for decades, but they have largely been ignored by advertisers. They know this, and it has steered them away from much of the current marketing tactics.

We will now journey into the essential spiritugraphic differences between this 38-million-household subgroup and the rest of American consumers. When we study the valuations of American households that have had a transformational spiritual experience and place it up against the views of the rest of the population, we will find tunnels into untapped mines of consumer loyalty. There are ways to engage with this powerhouse market that will cause them to listen where they otherwise haven't.

Setting aside whatever perspectives you have about faith and altruism in commerce, the first question you need to answer for your brand is, "How do I make money with this information?" A close second might be, "Is this a new market segment for me, or am I already engaging with this group of consumers?"

Spiritugraphics is a complement to demographics and psychographics. But spiritugraphics is more than an academic exercise or model. The findings related to this consumer segment are additionally beneficial if they can be leveraged into metrics that matter: reach, recall, net promoter scores, and market share are the key performance indicators for spiritugraphics.

Each spiritugraphic points to a perspective held by a segment of your audience. The trick is to activate the "Now what, so what?" of the observation, and then dial that idea up or down to serve the relationship between your brand and your targeted customer.

Each spiritugraphic points to a perspective held by a segment of your audience. The trick is to activate the "Now what, so what?" of the observation, and then dial that idea up or down to serve the relationship between your brand and your targeted customer. If you dial an idea too far in either direction, you're likely to find backlash and land mines that translate to less consumer engagement. If you dial it just right, you'll find treasures that have been hidden to you until today. As we introduce each spiritugraphic in the chapters to follow, we'll also provide the keys to activating these dials.

SPIRITUGRAPHICS CAN BE SYMBOLIC IN BRAND SIGNALING

For those of us working in brand management, we know symbols matter. That's because symbols are pointers. They come with meaning and backstory. And all public symbols have a variety of valid ways of being evaluated.

Consider the American flag. It is a symbol and its meaning is all about how it's presented. The same symbolism is true with each of the initial ten spiritugraphics. Our research has identified three layers of meaning for each.

First, in the case of the American flag, there's the *historical meaning*, with colonies, states, founding vision, and the records of battles won against historical figures and structures. The historical meaning of spiritugraphics is a matter of fact and is just the name of the symbol or observation. It is not part of how we'll be suggesting you leverage this content (more on that later).

Continuing the American flag example, next is the *aspirational meaning* that points beyond the flag itself to what we hope for in terms of liberty and justice for all. For our purposes, a negative response, say from Americans who see the flag as a symbol of a tyrannical past, is another form of aspirational meaning. The symbol itself elicits a particular response. This aspirational meaning is how you can dial up a given spiritugraphic perspective to connect with a segment by increasing contrast within the broader consumer market. In practical terms, anything you say directly and affirmatively about the American flag will elicit a positive response from some portion of your target audience and a potentially negative response from some other portion. Your brand wins based on how the blended or aggregate segments are tallied. In other words, when you win some, you may also lose some.

Finally, there is the merely *sentimental meaning*, which tends to play to a shared cultural experience the way a tattered flag or an old video clip of the flag in a gentle breeze might allude to a nonspecific American experience. This is how you can dial down a given spiritugraphic to appeal to a more general audience. You create context and a foundational background. Doing so allows you to pick battles and more effectively leverage and layer in other spiritugraphics to create the right recipe for your efforts.

There are all sorts of instances where a sentimental view on virtue is far more appropriate for the audience or the moment. And for every brand there will be spiritugraphic insights that resonate as core expressions for your offering, and then you'll have secondary and tertiary dials to refine. Sometimes setting these ancillary dials to sentimental rather than aspirational views of symbols allows you to extend simple invitations to celebrate everyday good things. In these instances, the topic is less combative and charged.

Brands generate affiliation and/or alienation with the aspirational claims they make about symbols such as the

American flag, while sentimental use of symbols creates a stable but generally undifferentiated backdrop for brand relationships. Compare this to how a marketer might use demographics and psychographics in an aspirational fashion as they market to men. They can do it in ways where the idea of masculinity is front and center, communicated directly, and where alignment with an expression of masculinity is how the brand is doing its work. Or consider how the same marketer might address the same male market segment in a sentimental fashion to present allergy medicine. They are communicating to a segment that happens to be male, but the call to action doesn't actively leverage manhood to drive behavior.

Sometimes the spiritugraphic provides the leverage for the call to action. Sometimes it provides the background where something else is meant to drive the response.

To put the example into practice, you could ask, "Is the American flag a useful symbol for my brand?" It depends on what you want to say about it and to whom.

What's useful to your brand is that you understand these symbols have meaning to the faith-driven consumers in your target audience. Then you can tailor your messages and delivery accordingly. Conversely, you'll want to understand what the symbols mean to your broader market. By netting these out, you can begin to set the dials across the nine spiritugraphics.

Any consumer can engage, and indeed has an ownership claim to, cultural traditions. But symbols are not weighted with the same meanings or significance for all people. Your mission as an effective marketer is to activate useful symbols and values with the right weight to

Your mission as an effective marketer is to activate useful symbols and values with the right weight to maximize positive responses from a targeted audience, without creating unwanted headwinds in the form of blowback from your other customers.

maximize positive responses from a targeted audience, without creating unwanted headwinds in the form of blowback from your other customers.

The following chapters are written with marketing leaders in mind. If that's you, here's an opportunity to think about how your team will respond to whatever you get from this spiritugraphic framework. If you lead a company, hopefully these findings unlock a new approach for your marketing team (and agency) to broaden the scope and connective tissue of your brand. If you see the value of what we're talking about, you'll need to be ready to lead the conversation with your team or client. (Or call us and we'll be more than happy to lead it for you.)

That should set the table. Now, let us show you the initial ten spiritugraphics that could influence and impact your market.

PART 2

Ten
Spiritugraphics

CHAPTER 6

Spiritugraphic #1: Relationship and Reputation

———

Born-again shoppers care deeply about connection. When they shop, it is seen as an extension of themselves and their core convictions. This means, in their eyes, even shopping transcends utility. This is one reason why the born-again shopper is concerned on a much higher level than the average American shopper with the character of the vendor receiving their business.

The born-again shopper is much more likely to desire access to a professional salesperson in-store and is also far more likely to recall experiencing great customer service. Connection and relationship with the vendor

———

The born-again shopper is concerned on a much higher level than the average American shopper with the character of the vendor receiving their business.

———

are high priorities to them on a human level. And when
the relationship and experience happen, they'll evangelize their newfound loyalty. It's the equivalent of going
viral in retail.

Born-again households were 21.2 percent more likely
than their counterparts to say that the reputation of a business was very important to them. This revelation extends
even beyond price point. If respondents specified that
reputation was very important to them, the survey asked a
follow-up question to gauge whether reputation was more
important than price.

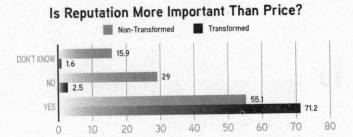

Is Reputation More Important Than Price?

The results show that born-again respondents were
over 15 percent more likely to value reputation even over
price compared to households that indicated it included a
person of faith but had not had a transformational spiritual
experience.

This emphasis on reputation finds itself married to
the born-again shopper's sensitivity for relationship and
connection, even regarding how they locate such a store.
Respondents who experienced a spiritual transformation
were 10 percent more likely to find such a store by asking a
friend or relative and 20 percent more likely to hear of such
a store from someone at church.

However, such valuations appear to extend beyond mere reputation. Born-again respondents were 30 percent more likely to make a special effort to find stores active in community programs compared to those who said they were a person of faith but were not classified as born-again.

Specifically, for born-again shoppers the event of shopping is less a solo enterprise and is far less about mere utility. For instance, it does not appear that a busy lifestyle is much of a threat to the shopping experience of a born-again shopper, compared to their counterparts.

Does a Busy Lifestyle Make Shopping Less Fun?

The born-again segment stated they were likely to shop alone, more likely to shop with family, and 18 percent less likely to feel that shopping takes too much time to do it often, compared to respondents who identify as people of faith who are not born-again.

In other words, for the born-again consumer shopping is an extension of themselves and their convictions. Where they shop and what they shop for says something about them. This is why they shop together and why they are happy to take their time; while shopping is enjoyable, it is still a commentary of their life. And when an ad man really thinks about this, it is excellent news! What marketing or advertising executive isn't looking for an intentional, passionate, and committed consumer? The born-again shopper is a largely untapped market, and—as the study reveals next—is a prime age to spend considerable amounts of money.

DECODING THE RELATIONSHIP AND REPUTATION SPIRITUGRAPHIC

How the Christian segment sees it: Relationships and reputations matter since every person bears the image of God and is immeasurably valuable because of God's defining role in creating us for human interaction.

The Aspirational dial: Use this dial to communicate how your brand celebrates human value and expressions of digity in ways that don't disregard or dishonor God and his authority as the basis for all life.

The Sentimental dial: Use this dial to highlight people and settings. Is it relationally driven to foster a connection of safety and care or are the actors and settings generic and transactional?

DIALING RELATIONSHIP AND REPUTATION UP AND DOWN

We're accustomed to seeing relationship messaging in play. Take the average pharmaceutical commercial that highlights a happy interaction between a trusted physician and an ailing patient. This level of trust is table stakes for any brand that promises medical care. A certain level of relational and reputational integrity *should* be assumed in settings where health and well-being are the focus.

The standard customer service win that you see so often, especially from health care and financial brands, is a conservative "make a person feel safe and cared for" sentimental route. The message is good but it's a background flavor rather than a genuine claim to value. In other words, does the pharma marketer have any choice but to exhibit trust?

For the born-again consumer shopping is an extension of themselves and their convictions. Where they shop and what they shop for says something about them.

In brand positioning and experience design, this spiritugraphic delivers free points most brands leave on the field because they don't have the language for what they're missing.

In terms of expressing love in relationship and reputation management, most brands can hit an aspirational "celebration of individual dignity" tone without turning anyone off depending on the accompanying illustrations and their meaning. If you're intentional about how you illustrate people and what other symbols you trigger, you can win significant points with the faith-based segment by asserting the idea that people bear the image of God, or at least hit some balance with a reference to "fearfully and wonderfully made" (Psalm 139:14), overlaying a wide variety of customer types.

> *You can win significant points with the faith-based segment by asserting the idea that people bear the image of God, or at least hit some balance with a reference to "fearfully and wonderfully made" (Psalm 139:14).*

A warning about being too on the nose with this one: if your industry already leads with the requirement of holding people in high esteem for how they're made (hospital, childcare, senior living, and so forth), you'll want to think about how you differentiate within your space. Your most likely recipe is to use this spiritugraphic as a background and then focus on some simple or practical differentiator in the actual customer experience you deliver.

EXPLORATION: RONALD BLUE TRUST

There may be no industry that struggles with differentiated or compelling messaging like financial planning and wealth management. The standard imagery and disclosures about past performance being no guarantee of future success are background noise at best. At worst, they're a missed opportunity to leverage a new segment that breaks away from the crowded category. The industry is so commoditized, conservative, and opaque to most consumers that it doesn't lend itself to great creative messaging.

The irony is that a remarkable percentage of wealth management practitioners approach their work with integrity and vision on par with nurses, social workers, and teachers (not to mention wealth managers have to answer for actual external performance metrics).

This statement of character is true in much of the industry, but it's highlighted in the practice of Ronald Blue Trust. Their approach boils down to three pillars: professional competence, principle alignment, and relational acumen.

First, the professional competence pillar is exceedingly difficult to address in meaningful ways in the abstract. And actual outcomes vary, in part because wealth management is a partnership process heavily influenced by personal choices and risk tolerances. In most ways professional competence, in the sense of bottom-line performance, is so difficult to prove that this pillar needs to be treated as something closer to a pass/fail fashion. This admission is no small task for professionals who constantly improve their skill sets and who understand the subtleties of their industry but must choose the lens of their customers. The lesson is universal: you are not your customer. You must be excellent at what you do, but sometimes vanilla is vanilla. Vanilla is important—you have to be

The lesson is universal: you are not your customer. You must be excellent at what you do, but sometimes vanilla is vanilla.

clear about what you're doing and how you're doing it—but when the thing you do is vanilla, you need a twist.

Second, the principle alignment pillar is the lynchpin and the twist for Ronald Blue Trust. Services need to line up with individuals' perspectives on money, legacy, generosity, risk, and personal guidelines. Clients who experience the best results with Ronald Blue Trust tend to be people who can agree with financial principles outlined in the Bible. This pillar is the lynchpin, but it is not what makes Ronald Blue Trust successful.

The more overt the respect and honor, the more sincere the love, the more the model delivers value.

What makes them successful is the third pillar: relational acumen. Once the technical requirements are clear, shared principles put the advisor and the client shoulder to shoulder to plan together. Anytime you can set the stage so you're seated on the same side of the table as your customer, good things will follow. Once you get the vanilla and the twist, all that matters is with whom you're going to enjoy it as you enjoy your ice cream. Ronald Blue Trust gets all of the buyer objections and pricing sorted out in the technical competence pillar, the shared vision and game plan defined within the principle alignment pillar, and from there the pressure is largely off . . . relational acumen carries the adventure from there.

Externalize the deliverable. Articulate and align on an approach. Let respect and honor take it from there. The more overt the respect and honor, the more sincere the love, the more the model delivers value. Some brands and industries might not appear to need to work this way, but it's hard to argue why they shouldn't.

CHAPTER 7

Spiritugraphic #2: Saying "Christmas"

O ne likely concern about the concept of spiritugraphics is the possibility that embracing such data could deter your current consumers and jeopardize market share. It's fair to ask if you're setting yourself up to lose more than you'd gain as you apply spiritugraphics in your messaging, creative, and marketing stack. However, you can often gain market share without losing much at all. Christmas is a perfect example.

When we asked respondents if the word "Christmas" affected their shopping habits, the response was nominally positive, though most respondents expressed indifference.

Are You More Likely to Purchase Products with "Christmas" in the Title?

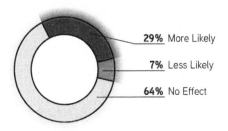

29% More Likely

7% Less Likely

64% No Effect

But guess which group was most responsible for the positive movement toward the word "Christmas" in their holiday shopping? If you guessed the born-again shopper, you would be correct.

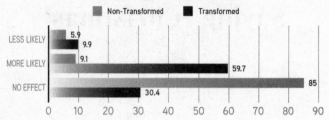

Are You More Likely to Purchase Products with "Christmas" in the Title?

This is a perfect example of how spiritugraphics is beneficial to market growth. Embracing the word (and associated imagery of) "Christmas" in holiday shopping is highly unlikely to negatively affect your fourth-quarter earnings. It could, however, boost holiday earnings due to the positive impact it will have on the born-again segment, for whom Christmas is a particularly significant time of year.

The holiday shopper is a "selective spender." They want each gift to count and each gift in the eyes of a born-again shopper should count.

Spiritugraphics during the holidays also give advertisers a leg up on understanding the economics of the holiday season. Specifically, spiritugraphics reveals a notable difference in how much the average household spends on Christmas each year.

How Much Do You Typically Spend on Christmas Gifts Each Year?

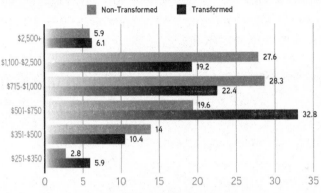

Legend: Non-Transformed, Transformed

Range	Non-Transformed	Transformed
$2,500+	5.9	6.1
$1,100-$2,500	27.6	19.2
$715-$1,000	28.3	22.4
$501-$750	19.6	32.8
$351-$500	14	10.4
$251-$350	2.8	5.9

Born-again households on average spend slightly less than other households during Christmas. This consumer behavior aligns well with the previously discussed discovery regarding born-again shoppers being less likely to have credit card debt. Born-again shoppers are thus more likely to shop within their means. However, this slight shift likely has to do with the fact that Christmas is more than a consumer holiday for the born-again household. Yet it would be a mistake to think that this means the born-again shopper is a frugal holiday shopper. Perhaps a better term would be that the holiday shopper is a "selective spender." They want each gift to count and each gift in the eyes of a born-again shopper should count.

Perhaps this is why the born-again holiday shopper is likely to spend more per gift. The most common price range per gift for the born-again shopper was fifty-one to seventy-five dollars, whereas the top price range per gift for those who did not record a transformational spiritual experience was thirty-six to fifty dollars. This indicates that overall born-again shoppers spend less on total gifts but more on each specific gift, a nod to quality over quantity. It also could be linked to the relational value this segment seeks during a thoughtful shopping season.

DECODING THE CHRISTMAS SPIRITUGRAPHIC
How the Christian segment sees it: Christmas celebrates the birth of Jesus, God in bodily form, here to pay the price of restoring communion between creation and Creator.

Aspirational dial: Use this dial to focus on joy, generosity, and reverent appreciation for God's gift, or at least offer a gesture toward the event and cause of the holiday.

Sentimental dial: Use this dial to focus on the American version of the holiday, with trees, presents, and the trappings of Christmas.

DIALING CHRISTMAS UP AND DOWN

The previous spiritugraphic about relationships and reputation is very broad, while this one comes down to if and how you consider deploying the single word "Christmas."

Where will you measure the value of your December campaign? If you're focused on a short-term sales bump, you're probably going to want the holiday to serve as backdrop and a little halo to your call to action. In that case, you stand to lose both the "Happy Holidays" crowd if you say "Christmas," and the "Merry Christmas" crowd if you say "Christmas" next to a too-transactional call to action. The obvious choice is to use the sentimental dial.

You can tune the aspirational dial and win broad approval if you point to what Christmas is supposed to be, holding up an inspiring version for your faith audience while demonstrating a more noble version of humanity to the rest of your market.

If you've concluded that your December campaign has more brand-building responsibility, you have more to consider. You can tune the aspirational dial and win broad approval if you point to what Christmas is *supposed* to be, holding up an inspiring version for your faith audience while demonstrating a more noble version of humanity to the rest of your market. If you put the Christmas idea as backdrop rather than superimposition, as in the story of a soldier returning to a faithful home with tree and trappings, a sentimental option will still get you favorably downstream with most audience segments.

EXPLORATION: STARBUCKS CUPS

There's something called a "virtuous circle," where one good thing gives rise to another good thing. Then there's a "virtue-signaling circle," where an arms race of moralizing leapfrogs into the abstract. The spiral of offense about Starbucks Christmas or holiday cups is a virtue-signaling circle. The person who doesn't want their cup to say "Christmas" triggers the person who's offended at the "persecution" they're facing when the word is expunged from their cup, and peppermint mocha gets more attention for it. Does the victory really matter to either side? And does either option on the December cups have a material result for Starbucks?

In truth, Starbucks has never used "Merry Christmas" on its cups, though you can buy a variety of Starbucks gift cards, ornaments, and Christmas-themed holiday products to suit your chosen position. In practice, the products on either side of this cultural battle are priced the same.

Starbucks seems to have concluded there's money to be made from Christmas-themed niche/peripheral products, but the trade isn't a great one for their brand affiliation and, therefore, their default offerings.

What about for your brand? It depends. Are you playing for the quick win or the long win? A Christmas bump that creates a lingering backlash is probably a bad idea. More importantly, every brand expression makes a brand promise, setting a customer expectation. Pick a side once and you'll be expected to keep picking it. For most brands, choosing a side defined by any entity outside of the brand is likely a fool's errand. Better not to start.

Far better is to determine what's true of your brand and say that in the affirmative, directly and without provocation. Virtue signaling can smell like manipulation and desperation and eventually leaves the brand signaler in a weak position.

CHAPTER 8

Spiritugraphic #3: Empty Nesters

———

Born-again shoppers maintain a strong relationship between their faith and their shopping. This connection leads to the type of consumer who prefers a shopping experience that is often shared and not rushed. Add to this equation a phase of life in which both adults often possess a working income and their children have left the home. Such a household has more time and more disposable income than previous generations. And this empty-nester segment isn't limited to the traditional retirement age; it's not uncommon for this broad group to include consumers in their forties and fifties. On the surface this is the empty-nester demographic. But there's also a spiritugraphic in play.

The first indicator that the born-again consumer represents a substantial piece of the empty-nester population can be realized by observing the age representation from our national behavioral study.

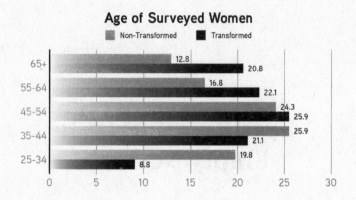

It is that simple. Born-again households make up more of the 45–54, 55–64, and 65-plus age brackets than their counterparts. The divergence only grows as the age ranges increase. This is a wealthy consumer with more time—and more shopping intent—than ever before.

A classic example of the power of the empty nester can be seen in the priorities of the American shopper. The clearest indicators of customer loyalty among empty nesters are ease of shopping and quality of product. The empty nester has time and money, but that time and money will not be wasted on a cumbersome shopping experience or on low-quality services. This stands in opposition to the priorities of their counterparts, who are far more likely to prioritize low price and variety of selection. When we take those trends and apply them to the empty nester, we are reminded that while an empty nester enjoys shopping, they are more likely to have an idea of what it is they want. This is why selection and price are of less importance.

However, there is one mistake marketers must not make when considering the female empty-nester

American consumer. This woman is not a disconnected, behind-the-times shopper. In fact, she is tech savvy and tends to supplement her affinity for shopping in-store with digital alternatives. Women are more likely to use their phones in-store to look up a discount or promotion code, or use their devices for a rewards program.

This is a simple way for advertisers to marry the ever-growing presence of tech in the shopping experience with those who prefer to shop in-store. The simple fact is that empty nesters prefer in-store shopping but probably have their phones out while doing so.

> *The clearest indicators of customer loyalty among empty nesters are ease of shopping and quality of product. The empty nester has time and money, but that time and money will not be wasted on a cumbersome shopping experience or on low-quality services.*

DECODING THE POWER OF EMPTY-NESTERS SPIRITUGRAPHIC

How the Christian segment sees it: Empty nesters have paid a price to offer a place of peace and protection for others, and they want to leave a legacy with their family and make a difference in the world.

Aspirational dial: Use this dial to celebrate the resources, shelter, and ability to offer the gifts of benevolence earned over the course of a long journey.

Sentimental dial: Use this dial to focus on the journey itself, not as a lost or fading memory, but as the construction of a credible living resume.

DIALING THE POWER OF EMPTY NESTERS UP AND DOWN

The difference between an aspirational expression and a sentimental expression is the difference between celebrating the price paid to accomplish something and romanticizing what older people used to look like when they were young and willing to pay the prices for their accomplishments. The aspirational signal honors and celebrates a success achieved on behalf of others. Brands harmonize with empty nesters when the heart of the value proposition is about *providing* something rather than *proving* something. It is about engaging a worthy expense for a worthy result to see the rewards for their efforts for how it impacts those they love. The wisdom evident in this spiritugraphic is similar to the wisdom of being a good passenger, a good patient, or a good member of a community, where aligning one's efforts with the force seeking your good makes everyone more successful.

EXPLORATION: COSTCO

In the ever-competitive brick-and-mortar chessboard, it's imperative for retailers to have a strong brand in play. They win by standing for something in the minds of their consumer. This positional game is heightened by the dominance of e-commerce and online shopping, which have the trump card for convenience as a strong value proposition. If convenience is off the table for traditional retail, what other brand attributes can retailers activate?

The task is even more important in business models that depend on annual memberships, such as Costco. The recurring membership is the epitome of lifetime value. This large wholesaler has built a brand tied to many attributes, but perhaps it is best known for utility, loyalty, and a positive customer experience.

These drivers are particularly relevant with the empty-nester segment. This group isn't looking for brands to tell them who they're going to be or how their lives are going to turn out. Empty nesters have a pretty good line on how their lives are unfolding. And whether they skew conservative or liberal, whether they're affluent or not (and this demographic is a whale in terms of spending power),

Brands harmonize with empty nesters when the heart of the value proposition is about providing *something rather than* proving *something. It is about engaging a worthy expense for a worthy result to see the rewards for their efforts for how it impacts those they love.*

what they're focused on is engaging the brands they need for the products or experiences they want with very little aspiration or ego as part of the equation. A credible brand, good prices, simple return policies, a known experience, and a little bit of whimsy in the form of an unanticipated item or offering, and an empty nester will respond with loyalty and enthusiasm. That's where Costco is winning with this spiritugraphic.

While Costco has something for everyone, the empty nester isn't relying on other attributes, such as fashion-forward clothing or a hip environment as a source of self-expression or a proxy for identity. Empty nesters already have answers. And from mundane, everyday shopping trips to grand adventures and indulgences, the key to engaging this spiritugraphic is to affirm the sense of self that exists in an empty nester and to connect your offering to the holistic ways they live out the conclusions they've earned.

> *From mundane, everyday shopping trips to grand adventures and indulgences, the key to engaging this spiritugraphic is to affirm the sense of self that exists in an empty nester, and to connect your offering to the holistic ways they live out the conclusions they've earned.*

This holistic approach has helped Costco hone a shopping experience for this segment. The wholesale brand has rounded out its offerings to include health and pharmacy services, travel planning and packages, and home services that are relevant to the empty nester's season in life. Any of these services is a business in its own right: Costco has masterfully woven these utilities under a singular brand promise of trust.

If your brand wants to engage the empty-nester spiritugraphic well, you could start by asking three fundamental questions about the selves the empty nesters have become:

1. What did they see when they finally saw beyond themselves?
2. What did that view inspire them to do in response?
3. How, or to whom, do the efforts of their lives deliver value today?

Your brand has empty nester possibilities if it points to something beyond itself, beyond the story of engaging your product or service and beyond the market in which you play, to meaning and substance that build value for the world and for the people your customers love. And if you can do it in a simple, matter-of-fact way, you'll win.

CHAPTER 9

Spiritugraphic #4: Made in America

———

When our survey asked women, "How much do you care if something you want is made out of the country?" overall, only 20.1 percent of respondents indicated that they cared very much. In fact, respondents were 16 percent more likely to indicate that they cared little to none (36.2 percent).

However, something significant happens when we compare responses to this question with whether a respondent has experienced a transformational spiritual experience.

How Much Do You Care if Something is Made Out of the Country?

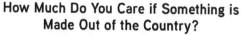

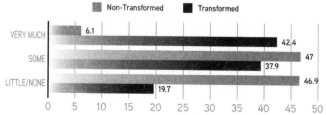

Over 80 percent of born-again respondents expressed at least some concern about a product's national origin, with the majority indicating that they care very much about where a product is made.

This is yet another example of the benefit of spiritugraphics: what is a neutral position for the average shopper is an area of considerable value for the born-again consumer. It's a dial worth tuning. By emphasizing "Made in America," one is likely to observe only a positive gain among this segment, with minimal risk of negative results in the broader market. Especially following a time when the average consumer has a heightened awareness of supply-chain disruption and economic uncertainty, the prospect of American-made products is likely to be viewed only in a positive light.

DECODING THE MADE IN AMERICA SPIRITUGRAPHIC

How the Christian segment sees it: Made in America is more than an ideal about a country's founding principles. It's also about loving your neighbor (and doing good by voting with your dollars in support).

Aspirational dial: Use this dial to celebrate the intrinsic rewards, trust, and discipline that accompanies the ideology of a national sovereignty (which is rooted in biblical foundations).

Sentimental dial: Use this dial to focus on the shared benefits and cultural artifacts of America, such as baseball, hot dogs, apple pie, and Chevrolet.

DIALING MADE IN AMERICA UP AND DOWN

This spiritugraphic is often seen in the wild as an aggressively sentimental tone that lands in the public square as tribalism. The genuine expression of this spiritugraphic is not macho; it's dedicated to service, obedience, and sacrifice, especially related to a protective and generous sort of gratitude.

There is a much more winsome version of Made in America that's been largely ignored and holds all sorts of power for all sides of the political spectrum. What's more, it holds its greatest leverage right on the cusp of maxed out aspirational expression. The short version is to focus not on a "we're great" sentiment of America, but on the underlying principles of serving something greater than yourself, offering a helping hand, and feeling part of a community.

EXPLORATION: KITCHENAID MIXERS

A strong Made in America brand is one that binds itself to a mission and a perspective that chooses to persist through generational trends, may well operate directly in the face of "common wisdom," and is willing to be proven right over a long-time horizon. It is distinct but not tribal, and tends to engage stakes that are too high to chase unproven or short-term market trends.

Obviously, you don't get to talk about "Made in America" until your product is made in America. But marketing is marketing. KitchenAid is part of Whirlpool, and both Whirlpool and KitchenAid have a deep portfolio that includes products that are imported. The KitchenAid mixer, though, is still a product of Greenville, Ohio. Other brands, such as your favorite chain saw or heavy-duty flashlight, are assembled in the United States and still find value in using marketing language tied to the "Built in America" tone.

These nuanced claims aside, it's clear brands want people to assume the words Made in America is short-hand for higher quality, better economic impact in the United States, and loyalty to American prosperity. That's not always the case. And for our purposes, even the literal coordinates of a product's origins are secondary.

What matters is what the product means on a symbolic level. New KitchenAid mixers look remarkably like old ones. Your kitchen will look and feel more like the kitchen of your youth. This emotional nod to adolescence is about familiarity and is an authentic expression that can't be manufactured. The mixer stands for home cooking in an era of carryout, deliveries, and microwaves. The design is an expression of classical pragmatism and is generally a thoughtful addition to a wedding registry. The symbols of this spiritugraphic make promises about enduring quality, staying the course, and "leaving the light on." What could be more American-made than these sincere expressions?

CHAPTER 10

Spiritugraphic #5: Small-Town Ideals

A s John Mellencamp would say, "Yeah, I can be myself here in this small town / and people let me be just what I want to be."[81] He was on to something when he penned these lyrics for they are stunningly accurate in describing the behaviors of the born-again consumer. Our study carved out an intentional segment of questions geared toward measuring the environment of one's upbringing. The population of a consumer's hometown was the first such question posed.

What Was the Population of Where You Grew Up

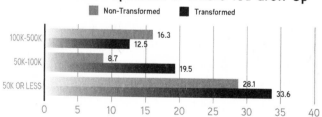

The results are quite telling. A trend toward small-town roots emerges in the born-again segment. Households that indicated experiencing a spiritual transformation were over 16 percent more likely than their spiritual counterparts to have grown up in a town of fewer than 100,000 people. Not only were born-again respondents more likely to come from a smaller town, they were also more likely to have remained in their small-town environment.

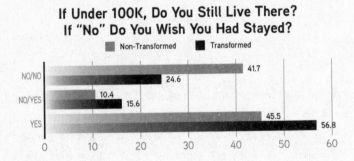

If Under 100K, Do You Still Live There?
If "No" Do You Wish You Had Stayed?

■ Non-Transformed ■ Transformed

NO/NO — 41.7 / 24.6
NO/YES — 10.4 / 15.6
YES — 45.5 / 56.8

Born-again respondents were 10 percent more likely to have stayed in their small town and were also more likely to have wished they stayed if they did leave. Notice, also, that respondents who did not experience a spiritual transformation were significantly more likely both to have left their small-town home and to have not wished they'd stayed.

This loyalty to one's original home is once again evident in the shopping habits of the born-again household. Sixty-six percent of born-again respondents indicated they try to buy from neighborhood, locally owned stores, more than the average American shopper. This makes sense in a context where the born-again shopper is more likely to have an authentic relationship with the owner of the store in which they shop. Such roots of familiarity and loyalty are indeed deep.

DECODING THE SMALL-TOWN VALUES SPIRITUGRAPHIC

How the Christian segment sees it: Small-town values are about freedom and liberty while extending grace and staying connected to the community.

Aspirational dial: Use this dial to celebrate the extension of kindness, generosity, and space for the needs and wishes of others.

Sentimental dial: Use this dial to focus on the nostalgia and pride of trusting brands that speak to one's familiarity and personal connection.

DIALING SMALL-TOWN VALUES UP AND DOWN

This spiritugraphic dial can be a challenge to tune. Marketers tend to choose clichés, yet there are options that can perform far better to a far broader audience. This is another example where an aspirational expression gets you better results.

The shorthand for Small Town Values could be "love looks like something." This is even more amplified in traditional small-town settings where participants operate under the norms of transparency and intimacy in their personal business and life's details (even when they don't ask for it to be public knowledge).

The difference between a strong brand association and a weak brand expression with Small Town Values is the difference between inspiring kindness (which is easy) and demanding it (which is impossible). It's also important to note that "small town" doesn't have to be the literal size of a geography. These expressions can exist in big-city context: neighborhood bodegas and street-inspired brands know this recipe well.

EXPLORATION: CRACKER BARREL

This three-billion-dollar company is frequented by the 18–29 crowd at an even higher rate than the 50–65 crowd, with the 30–49 demographic coming in slightly behind the other two. Turns out, the net promoter score and customer loyalty numbers put Cracker Barrel in the top of its category. And as much as the decor may convey a more conservative than progressive vibe, the brand is seen as socially neutral. Cracker Barrel isn't winning because of basic demographic courtship. It's winning because the business is built to leverage a spiritugraphic insight: people respond to kindness and community and a romantic view of hometown welcome.

Over 33 percent of Cracker Barrel customers visit the stores while traveling. And what they experience isn't about fashion, coolness, health, speed, or self-expression. What they experience is a sense of welcome like they might receive from a sweet, attentive, and traditionally selfless aunt. Cracker Barrel customers certainly may echo the brand sentiment of the business, and they may affiliate with it, but Cracker Barrel is not a brand for the ambitious ego; it's a microeconomy of kindness where company and customers seem to agree to put aside whatever differences they may have in more selfish moments and focus instead on a simple, delicious meal and sense of welcome as they go.

Call it a choice not to worry about "all that big-city stuff." Call it a moment of rural sanctuary. Call it a narrow focus with simple rules of hospitality. It's kindness offered in a specific manner, unselfconscious and unpresuming and all too rare in a world of frantic signaling and missing the people who are the point. It's enough to create and hold the space; customers reward such behavior. With this market, good brands don't require extra credit for doing the right thing.

It's kindness offered in a specific manner, unselfconscious and unpresuming and all too rare in a world of frantic signaling and missing the people who are the point. It's enough to create and hold the space; customers reward such behavior.

CHAPTER 11

Spiritugraphic #6: Lent

Households that indicated they had a transformational spiritual experience were over 20 percent more likely to change their behavior (specifically, their diet) in observation of Lent—the period on the Christian calendar between Ash Wednesday and Easter.

Regarding the most popular items to give up for Lent, even more disparity was captured between born-again respondents and their counterparts.

If Yes, What Do You Avoid for Lent?

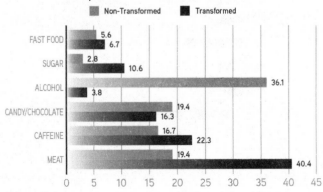

This proclivity for one group of respondents to avoid alcohol for Lent and the other to not is telling of another difference of habit— born-again Christians are significantly less likely to consume alcohol.

Meat is the overwhelmingly common Lenten sacrifice among born-again respondents, followed by caffeine as a distant second. Conversely, among those who have not indicated a transformational spiritual experience—a group significantly unlikely to practice Lent to begin with—alcohol is the overwhelmingly popular item to abstain from, followed distantly by meat and candy.

This proclivity for one group of respondents to avoid alcohol for Lent and the other to not is telling of another difference of habit— born-again Christians are significantly less likely to consume alcohol.

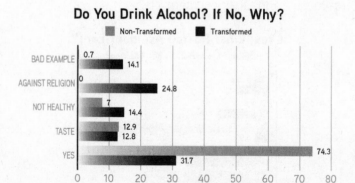

Do You Drink Alcohol? If No, Why?

Even more telling than the aversion to drinking alcohol is the reasoning for not drinking alcohol among those who abstain. Just under 25 percent of born-again respondents who indicated they do not drink alcohol cited their religion as the reason why they do not, compared to none of their counterparts. The religious reasoning for such conviction is tethered to the position within the Christian worldview to view the body as a vessel for God. One will often hear a Christian state something to the extent of "my body is a temple." This motivation drives the hesitancy toward alcohol and also speaks to the larger concept of Lent. The person of faith is withholding what is common from the body in order to achieve deeper intimacy with God.

Applying spiritugraphics with an awareness of this discipline unlocks new avenues for market growth. All that is needed is an understanding of how faith informs habits in the born-again consumer.

DECODING THE LENT SPIRITUGRAPHIC

How the Christian segment sees it: Lent is an expression of faith in response to a God who is the supreme model of faithfulness. Lenten sacrifices are an expression of obedience.

Aspirational dial: Use this lever to celebrate—anytime of year—any behavior that is born from a faithful and loving devotion to God or a person's covenants with others.

Sentimental dial: Use this lever to focus—anytime of year or among any group of people—on the traditions pinned to a particular group of people.

DIALING LENT UP AND DOWN

This one is free money for anyone who wants it. Where Christmas is ubiquitous and often secular, Lent is more peripheral and there's almost zero resistance to leveraging it, even from tangential consumer segments. What's more, there are thousands of options for engaging Lent, for pursuing connection with God, by making conscious buying or giving behaviors and finding healthy ways of making spiritual choices without adopting an overtly religious posture or position. Caffeine-free soda and pressed juice mocktails have wide appeal in their own right, but they can have an amplified reach within this market segment.

Even beyond Lent, there is a vision for faithfulness in action that rewards biblical rather than traditional responses. Brands can harmonize with this when they speak to "the things you do because of the things you stand for and what they say about you."

This is such untapped space that there are very few brands that couldn't win significant ground here.

EXPLORATION: CARHARTT

The spirit of Lent is not limited to the forty-day period celebrated by a subset of Christians. It is also about a posture of faithfulness applied in the form of personal sacrifice for the sake of love and growth. When personal sacrifice is shared with others who hold a similar posture, the community experiences a level of camaraderie, a language for appreciation, and a sharpened focus on the point of adoration that defines the whole.

Consider Carhartt and the workers who arise before dawn and bundle up in the brand's tough clothing to labor in service of their trade. Carhartt still makes clothing worn by people who do the sorts of things illustrated in their marketing. And that clothing has earned the loyalty of people who value their money for practicality and lifestyle durability.

The Carhartt customer, the early morning skilled worker with mud on their boots, is where the Lent marker truly lives. It's their lifestyle and consistent choices that set the tune with which Carhartt harmonizes. But the company makes its own sacrifices, beyond building with quality, to live its brand.

Carhartt had donated hundreds of thousands of dollars to educate and train America's future workforce.[82] This

When personal sacrifice is shared with others who hold a similar posture, the community experiences a level of camaraderie, a language for appreciation, and a sharpened focus on the point of adoration that defines the whole.

If you can find that inspiration, that vision worth suffering to achieve, and if you can connect that inspiration with your brand so that your brand becomes a reminder of a desire that transcends a moment's consumption, you have the basis for a strong Lent dial.

is part of an ongoing series of efforts and partnerships to close the skilled trades gap. Such is the appreciation for the Lent-like persistent sacrifices of its customer base.

What does your brand invite consumers to own, engage, celebrate, and sacrifice to pursue? If you can find that inspiration, that vision worth suffering to achieve, and if you can connect that inspiration with your brand so that your brand becomes a reminder of a desire that transcends a moment's consumption, you have the basis for a strong Lent dial.

CHAPTER 12

Spiritugraphic #7: Not-So-New Media

Another commonly held belief assumed to be inevitable for the last several years is the notion that Americans are no longer watching as much television, and that the inevitable move toward streaming across other devices is underway.

Yet our study revealed that the opposite is true. When asked if they or their family are watching more or less television over the past few months, a majority of respondents indicated they are watching more, not less. When the study sought to elaborate on what they are watching more of, the results were interesting.

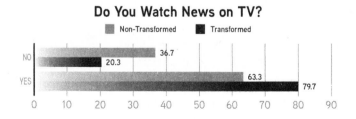

Do You Watch News on TV?

Despite the belief that Americans no longer get their news from mainstream media, the data suggests a large majority of Americans still do.

Despite the widely held belief that Americans are no longer getting their news from the mainstream media, the data suggests a large majority of Americans still do. We also find that cable news—specifically Fox News—dominates the airwaves.

Our agency clients have benefited from this reality, as many of our faith-conscious brands require nuance in getting airtime and ad placement. Yet they've found welcomed space on Fox News and other cable news networks, often with exceptional results.

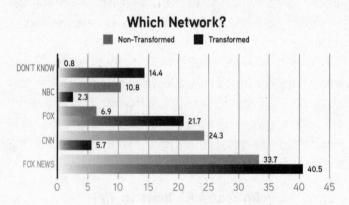

Which Network?

Our clients have also enjoyed brand safety and reach with Food Network. This was also backed by our study findings. When asked what families are watching more of over the past few months, an interesting divergence occurred.

What Type of Programming Are You Watching More?

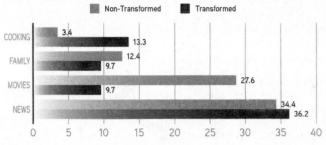

Non-Transformed   Transformed

COOKING — Non-Transformed 3.4, Transformed 13.3
FAMILY — Non-Transformed 12.4, Transformed 9.7
MOVIES — Non-Transformed 27.6, Transformed 9.7
NEWS — Non-Transformed 34.4, Transformed 36.2

Cooking appears to be the area where born-again viewers are gravitating beyond the news. Our agency has embraced this seemingly odd divergence in media and brand planning. Suffice to say, our faith-forward clients have enjoyed gains in engagement and market share through Food Network placement and campaigns. These networks are masterful using cross-channel communications, allowing marketers to truly meet this segment where they are—whether that's television, mobile, social, or email.

All in all, it would appear that, like Mark Twain's death, the reports of television's death are greatly exaggerated. Advertisers have found fertile ground with the opportunity for positive yields through cable networks—especially if the content is geared toward news or food/cooking. It is unusual to consider the religious consumer as a leader in advertising trends, but this might be an example of just that.

DECODING THE NOT-SO-NEW MEDIA SPIRITUGRAPHIC

How the Christian segment sees it: The call to offer one another a meaningful place of gentle hope and sanctuary

requires us to trust God's paradigm over culture's obses-
sion with media influencers.

Aspirational dial: Use this lever to celebrate laying aside
self and personal prerogatives for the sake of humbly
nurturing relationships and expressions of peace.

Sentimental dial: Use this lever to focus on culture as a
safe place of self-expression and diversity for its own sake.

DIALING NOT-SO-NEW MEDIA UP AND DOWN

Marshall McLuhan was right when he said, "The medium
is the message." New media, social media, a medium of
accessible, disposable, scrolling projections of filtered
selves and memes, not only tend to define the messages
that suit the medium, but the medium itself conveys a critical message about what matters and how people should
measure their own life's worth.

This chaos in public discourse lacks the footholds required for a useful expression of peace where people are actually honored and protected. And for whatever complaints your faith-based audience has about new media, there's a chance they've played a contributing role in its highly engaging and consumptive social platforms.

The question for you and your brand is this: Is there greater gain playing into the chaos with a sentimental position? Or would your brand be better served by inviting people to "eddy out" of the sweeping currents into either a better rule set or an intentional break from snack media for something closer to a meal with substance?

EXPLORATION: MAGNOLIA NETWORK

The rise of Chip and Joanna Gaines is well-documented. From the early days of *Fixer Upper*, the home renovation series, it was clear this likable couple was more than do-it-yourselfers: they were on a path to media domination.

It's hard to specifically categorize all the Gaines empire has to offer. With each passing season the brand seemingly adds offerings with ease—TV hosts, product designers, retailers, authors, and broadcast entrepreneurs all fit the bill describing these moguls. While any of these labels suits them, much of their underlying business brand points to media. This fun-loving Waco, Texas, duo has built more than a niche; they've built a following by activating brand signals that connect with a large swath of cable, social, and digital media audiences.

Take the Magnolia Network property. No question, this umbrella brand has a symbiotic relationship with the original "Chip and Jo" personalities (and also with their farmhouse-inspired design and lifestyle aesthetic). The network is a natural extension of the brand. It makes their audience feel, and often legitimately become, more mean-ingfully engaged in inspired ideas to improve how they live. This is best illustrated in Magnolia's "We believe in home" manifesto, which offers a proclamation perfectly suited for spiritugraphics:

> Throughout all the joys and challenges that life brings, home always seems to be right in the middle of it. It's what catches us, and also what lifts us up. It's where we retreat, where we are restored, and also where we bring our community together to share a meal at the table
>
> But we've learned that home doesn't have to be a physical destination. Any place you feel known, loved, and always welcomed back is a home of its own.
>
> We believe these things so deeply that every-thing we do at Magnolia is in pursuit of inspiring people to create a home and a life they love. And whether you find us mostly online or at the Market here in Waco, inside the pages of our magazine or on the shows of Magnolia Network, it is our ongoing desire that any time you spend with us will help guide you there.[83]

Magnolia has masterfully activated the very insights covered in previous chapters. From featuring "Christmas" recipes to personifying Waco's "small town ideals" to encouraging "relationships" through group shopping at the Silos retail experience, Magnolia has reached the matters of the soul (i.e., spiritugraphics) in a meaningful way with consumers.

The Magnolia brand demonstrates the medium can in fact be the message. When the network uses the promise of delivering inspiration and restoration through various media channels, not only has the brand laid claim to something as sacred as our home space, it's made a promise to work from a mindful, purposeful, and life-giving posture about truth as the brand finds it. Spoiler alert: It's not really about your house and home. It's far more about living, connecting, and being inspired. Within that promise, the Gainses aren't bashful about their faith, but they've never made their work overtly or exclusively about faith. Their dial is tuned for wide appeal, and they've benefited from not catering to, or alienating, any particular market segment. The magazine, design blog, social images, and recipes aren't exclusively about faith. But the markers are there.

When the network uses the promise of delivering inspiration and restoration through various media channels, not only has the brand laid claim to something as sacred as our home space, it's made a promise to work from a mindful, purposeful, and life-giving posture about truth as the brand finds it.

Done well, a Not-So-New Media brand can absolutely embrace new and social media. What will set the brand apart is if it has a bigger idea, something beyond itself it cares about and to which it steers others—not in the form of a series of bandwagon campaigns, but as a theme and a refrain through which people can see deeper, longer, or wider in some worthy manner.

CHAPTER 13

Spiritugraphic #8:
Old-School Values

———

It would not be inaccurate for the born-again consumer to be considered a bit of an "old soul" for reasons beyond just media consumption and in-person shopping preferences. Corresponding behavior among households reporting an experience of spiritual transformation further supports this old-school, old soul dynamic. One such example is the topic of tattoos.

Have You Ever Considered Getting a Tattoo?

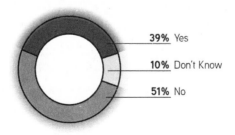

39% Yes

10% Don't Know

51% No

Notice that of all women surveyed—spirituality aside—over half have never even considered getting a tattoo. Ironically, when we return to our common dichotomy of comparing people of faith who have or have not had a transformational spiritual experience, we see an increased consideration of tattoos in women who consider themselves a person of faith but have not had a transformational spiritual experience. Women with no religious identity are less likely than the nominal woman of faith to consider getting a tattoo. The same cannot be said for the born-again household.

Have You Ever Considered Getting a Tattoo?

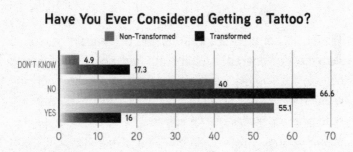

In fact, born-again women are nearly 22 percent more likely to cite a faith-driven reason for not getting a tattoo than their counterparts. What is the motivation against considering tattoos for born-again women? The answer lies in one's worldview regarding the body. A born-again individual is more likely to cite the notion that their body is a temple of the Lord's, and is thus going to be far more conservative toward what they ingest and how they adorn their bodies. This has already been made clear in the born-again attitude toward alcohol and clothing. Thus the behavior away from considering tattoos is rather predictable.

Similar trends are revealed concerning body piercings (excluding ear piercings). Placing spirituality aside for a moment, only 41 percent of all women have considered a body piercing.

Have You Ever Considered a Body Piercing?

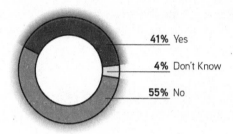

41% Yes

4% Don't Know

55% No

This means a majority of all women surveyed have not considered body piercing, and yet when spirituality is examined in this context, a familiar trend reappears. A woman who considers herself a person of faith but who has not had a transformational spiritual experience shows a higher likelihood of considering a body piercing than the average woman.

Have You Ever Considered a Body Piercing?

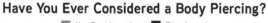

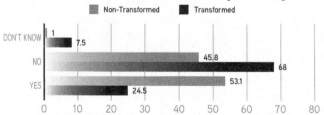

On the other side of the spectrum, born-again respondents were 13 percent more likely not to consider a body piercing than the average woman. As well, born-again households were nearly 23 percent more likely to cite their reason not to consider a body piercing as being faith-driven.

You might be asking, "What do tattoos, piercings, and other matters of the body have to do with marketing?" These findings not only give us additional insight into how this segment views themselves but also provide guidance on how to portray the cast in your brand's production. Whether it's stock photography or actor portrayals, body art and choices can connect (or disconnect) with this segment quickly.

DECODING THE OLD-SCHOOL SPIRITUGRAPHIC

How the Christian segment sees it: Self-control urges people to choose against immediate gratification with this choice being a tribute to God, whose presence makes this life and the next far more rewarding.

Aspirational dial: Use this lever to celebrate freedom *to*—to follow, to obey, to honor, to serve, and to live as a blessing to others in response to a calling.

Sentimental dial: Use this lever to focus on freedom *from*—from want, from pain, from consequences, from being small or not the center of one's world.

DIALING OLD SCHOOL UP AND DOWN

There's a strong sentimental dial with this spiritugraphic, largely defined in today's market by messages against old-school thinking as repressive and unenlightened. This is the inevitable conclusion of a century of marketing that followed a potent four-point recipe: (1) consumers of any given product or category can be defined by a specific addressable pain, (2) pain is bad and unwanted, (3) pain is optional to the extent that the right product or service can eliminate the pain, and (4) pain is shameful in the sense that if it's bad and optional but shows up anyway, it reflects negatively on the person who experiences the pain.

This dynamic is so pervasive that it's no longer pain itself that drives the economy so much as it is the associated fear of it (as evidenced by Cesar Millan's enterprise derived from teaching people to walk their dogs in such a way that strangers driving by might not judge them harshly for doing it wrong). The messaging of the last century drove people into smaller and smaller personal spaces, down into smaller rewards and more market-consumer-generated fears to a place where even the *freedom from* brand position sounds rather aspirational.

But there is a significant difference between freedom *from* some external friction and freedom *to* pursue something higher. The trick to a better sort of life, even if it comes with additional friction, is embracing an adventure worth suffering for. Those adventures happen only when a person falls in love with something bigger than themself and when a brand does the same, pointing to a vision beyond the customer and beyond the provider—to a destination worth pursuing together.

EXPLORATION: THE UNITED STATES MARINES

The only branch of the United States military that consistently meets its recruiting goals is the Marine Corps. Their basic brand premise is that *it's going to be really tough (but if you can handle it, you'll have social proof for life that you're among an elite group).*

The trick to a better sort of life, even if it comes with additional friction, is embracing an adventure worth suffering for.

The Marines, and other disciplined mission-driven adherents, authentically believe in the value of the mission, the destination toward which they're headed, and the value of the invitation they extend to others. This high-performing group hears phrases such as "YOLO—you only live once," and respond with, "That's right—what are you going to spend it on?"

Commitment is a reflection of a person's clarity regarding something for which they're willing to make self-sacrifices. That self-sacrifice is the affirmative RSVP to an adventure that's worth suffering to take, and the payoffs are rarely clear at the starting line. That, of course, is where brand positioning has an impact.

What adventure does your brand point to that's worth suffering to engage? What pain does your brand invite someone to consider and pay to get somewhere with you? What vision has so captivated your company that you're paying to respond in service of that vision? When you can name those things, you can engage old-school commitment levers and provide a compelling alternative to today's default market of self-gratification and loyalty-less, appetite-driven selfishness, which is far easier to compete against.

CHAPTER 14

Spiritugraphic #9: Daughters Are Different

One of the most interesting aspects of our study was revealed when the survey questioned mothers of daughters. Fascinatingly, these mothers acknowledged a simple truth across all ideologies—in the eyes of all mothers, daughters are simply different.

There are many reasons why daughters may face a different sort of review and hear a different sort of guidance from their mothers. Girls face different social dynamics. They also face different physical risks and social prejudices at every turn. There are ways in other relationships that mothers and daughters reflect upon each other, where mothers have an easier time if the daughter is kept within more protective bounds. The simple reality is that women are often seen in a more sexualized and objectified fashion than men, and it would be no surprise to learn mothers prefer to delay that reality for their daughters as long as they can. Maybe it's old-fashioned and unfair, but maybe among the faith-led crowd there is something else at play. First, the results:

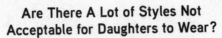

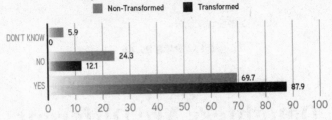

A heavy majority of all households affirmed this sensitivity toward their daughters' attire. Predictably, this sensitivity led to preventative action in a majority of households. In fact, born-again households and their counterparts were equally likely to have prevented their daughter from buying a garment they believed was too revealing.

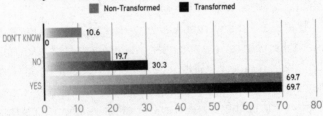

However, the explanation behind the preventative action is where the divergence is revealed. For a born-again household, this is a matter of faith in over half of the cases. For households not indicating a transformational spiritual experience, faith was the explanation for preventing their daughter from buying a too-revealing garment in just over 3 percent of cases.

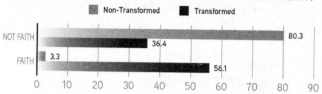

Did You Restrict These Items Based on Your Faith?

This divergence is significant, because religious conviction appears to persist in other areas such as dress length and swimming attire.

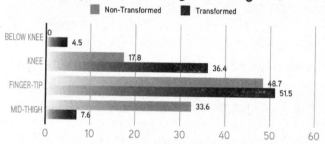

Appropriate Dress Length for Daughters

While born-again households and their counterparts are all most likely to agree that a fingertip-length dress is the ideal length, the two spiritugraphics move in opposite directions from this middle-ground position. Born-again households gravitate toward knee-length dresses, and their counterparts toward mid-thigh. Of course, school dress codes can be a neutralizing factor across the broader consumer market.

However, there's much less consensus pertaining to swimwear. Born-again households indicated little flexibility beyond a one-piece, whereas their counterparts were far more likely to express flexibility across various options.

Appropriate Swimsuit for Daughters

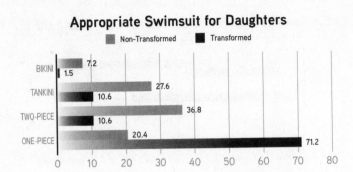

Religious conviction as a point of divergence is far more likely to extend from emphasis on daughters into practical application for the respondent herself. When questions turned away from daughters and toward one's opinion regarding their own clothing, the born-again household was more likely to operate in concert with how they parent their daughters. Consider, for instance, how households responded to questions pertaining to skirt lengths today.

Do You Worry About How Short Women's Skirts Are Today? If Yes, What is Appropriate?

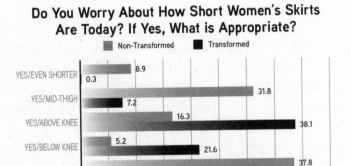

Born-again women are more likely to show concern for skirt length, and more likely to believe a longer skirt is appropriate. This same attitude extends to women's tops as well.

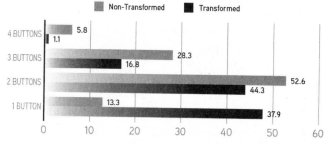

How Many Buttons Should Be Unbuttoned for a Blouse to Be Appropriate?

Much like all mothers were in agreement that a daughter's dress should be fingertip in length, most women in the survey settled on two buttons unbuttoned as most appropriate on a blouse. Yet again, however, one's spiritual experience caused two divergent movements. The second most common answer among born-again respondents was one button, while the second most common answer among those who did not record a transformational spiritual experience was three buttons.

These responses are fascinating, especially in light of the dominant expressions of dress for women in pop culture today. The dress of America's most visible women betrays the viewpoints of most women in the study; it's even more so for born-again women.

DECODING THE DAUGHTERS ARE
DIFFERENT SPIRITUGRAPHIC

How the Christian segment sees it: Daughters represent a particular hope about life, vitality, and proximity to an innocence demonstrated in the God who gives life.

Aspirational dial: Use this lever to celebrate an unhurried, unconsumed, unobjectified, unclaimed hope for joy and goodness as the girl pursues life.

Sentimental dial: Use this lever to focus on universal and untainted coming-of-age experiences driven from within rather than from externalized identity benchmarks.

DIALING DAUGHTERS ARE
DIFFERENT UP AND DOWN

If the secret when talking about empty nesters is to focus on where they are and what they've achieved today rather than romanticizing where they were long ago, the secret to daughters (and sons) is to focus on where they are today rather than defining them against where they're headed. Did the work of the empty nester matter? Does the innocence of a child? Neither group is seen or honored well by defining it against the consumption, chaos, and self-absorption of the middle years.

The question is not about buying behavior. There are ways to influence that by underscoring the preservation of innocence and the celebration of youthful vitality. The question has far more to do with whether the sentimental brand options focus on consumption, not just of products and services, but of hearts and childhoods.

If the secret when talking about empty nesters is to focus on where they are and what they've achieved today rather than romanticizing where they were long ago, the secret to daughters (and sons) is to focus on where they are today rather than defining them against where they're headed.

EXPLORATION: IVORY SOAP

Ivory has been dialed in on this spiritugraphic since the 1940s. The accent has changed over the decades, from gentleness and purity, to a mix of self-care and financial consciousness, to a down-to-basics refusal of artificiality, to sharing personal wisdom with the whole family. But the basic idea has always been a celebration of healthy vitality and feminine wisdom.

Ivory has always found copy and visuals that move into intimate but ordinary places. Private thoughts or worries, daily chores, shower and bath scenes, feedback from husbands, simple conversations with children. But what makes it work is a validation and affirmation of women, based not on the response they get but on the way they feel and make choices regarding the things they care about.

What makes it work is a validation and affirmation of women, based not on the response they get but on the way they feel and make choices regarding the things they care about.

Ivory Soap has been a safe presence in those moments. It hasn't sexualized or consumed, it hasn't urged an agenda beyond the everyday aspirations of its customer, and it hasn't betrayed that trust by making intimate moments something they aren't—these sentiments breed an uncommon level of trust for, and community around, the brand. Of course, this isn't entirely by accident, evidenced by the soap brand's underlying mission and vision statement: "For 133 years, we have continued to innovate Ivory to remain an effective, yet gentle everyday cleanser for the entire family at a great value. It may be a simple formula, but staying true to this promise has kept Ivory pure, clean and gentle for seven generations."[84]

Gentle. Pure. Safe. This lexicon is a near endorsement of the Daughters Are Different spiritugraphic.

How would Ivory Soap manage a preteen clothing line? How would Ivory manage your brand when it comes to the way your brand shows up in family contexts and intimate moments? What might your brand gain by dialing up the goodness factor in your messages?

CHAPTER 15

Spiritugraphic #10: Not Yet Woke

Woke culture is part of the advertising discussion. This is especially evident in the way major corporations utilize ad space to take different stances on the various social issues of our time. If one studied only the nature of these advertising campaigns, the following breakdown of political affiliation in America might be surprising.

Political Philosophy

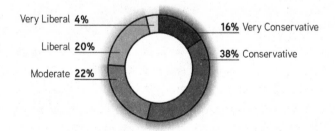

Very Liberal **4%**

Liberal **20%**

Moderate **22%**

16% Very Conservative

38% Conservative

This breakdown does not account for any spiritual designation among the thousand women who took the survey, and yet 54 percent of participants reported a right-leaning, conservative ideology. When one adds the 22 percent of respondents who identify as moderate, this does not leave a large piece of the pie for the aggressive, left-leaning social advertisements that often run on the airwaves. This suggests that such efforts are at best tolerated by a majority of the population. Now, when spirituality is accounted for, one finds another looming spiritugraphic.

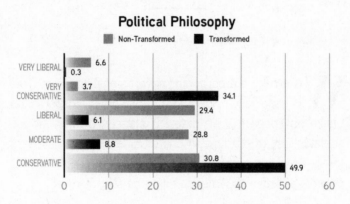

Born-again consumers are 84 percent likely to lean conservative in their political ideology. The implications of this are notable. Whereas a decent chunk of the population might tolerate woke-inspired marketing efforts, the born-again population is likely far less willing to brush such tactics aside as a consumer.

One such case study would be the topic of LGBTQ rights. Consider, for instance, the overall results of America's Research Groups National Behavioral Study toward the topic of gay marriage.

Opinion Related to Gay Marriage

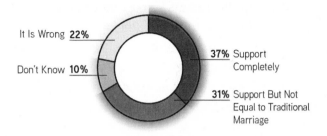

It Is Wrong **22%**

Don't Know **10%**

37% Support Completely

31% Support But Not Equal to Traditional Marriage

This breakdown of one thousand women—spirituality temporarily put aside—reveals a similar attitude shown in the previous findings on political ideology. Complete support of gay marriage represents less than 40 percent of the survey. However, nearly another third of the poll expresses a healthy tolerance of the notion. But what happens when we cross-reference this issue with spirituality?

Opinion Related to Gay Marriage

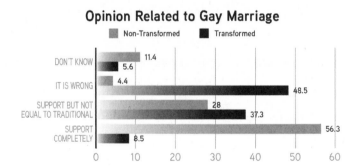

Non-Transformed   Transformed

DON'T KNOW — 11.4 / 5.6

IT IS WRONG — 4.4 / 48.5

SUPPORT BUT NOT EQUAL TO TRADITIONAL — 28 / 37.3

SUPPORT COMPLETELY — 56.3 / 8.5

Born-again respondents are very unlikely to offer complete support, and nearly half express a moral concern toward gay marriage. What does this have to do with consumer habits of the American shopper? The answer is enveloped in the trends of some corporations to marry a social issue with their marketing efforts. Many advertisers incorporate LGBTQ support into their marketing efforts. The question as it pertains to this study, then, is how much net gain or loss does such an effort wield? The survey asked just such a question to the thousand women who participated in the study.

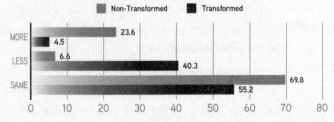

Are You More/Less Likely to Shop at Target Due to Its Support of Gay/Lesbian Rights?

Whatever gains a brand might earn from advertising their support of this cultural topic is significantly eclipsed by the losses felt by losing a significant segment of the population.

It would be foolish to believe that this isn't a sensitive and highly charged topic, but if one looks at this data from a position of market valuation, a compelling data point emerges. Whatever gains a brand might earn from advertising their support of this cultural topic is significantly eclipsed by the losses felt by losing a significant segment of the population.

Born-again shoppers are notably less likely to advocate for a brand that publicly supports LGBTQ rights, and the brand's stance does not affect other consumers enough to make a difference either way. Thus, indexing or focusing on the topic could adversely affect customer acquisition, retention, and share of wallet.

A similar trend is visible as it pertains to brands (stores) that publicly support the Black Lives Matter movement.

Are You More/Less Likely to Shop at Stores in Favor of Black Lives Matter?

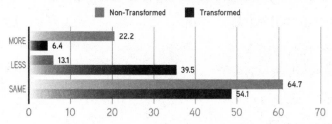

In fact, the results are wildly close to the data gathered on LGBTQ support. As a marketer, a key question you should be asking is related to math. Aside from declaring a social position, does the calculus of advertising on key issues provide a net return? The study indicates those who consciously patronize a brand because of their support for Black Lives Matter is eclipsed by those who will consciously avoid the store for the same reason.

These are undoubtedly loaded topics for any business conversation, but the influence of social causes on advertising can't be ignored. Certainly, an entirely different book could be dedicated to the divergence of worldviews between born-again Christians and others; indeed, at least one such book already exists.[85] It is pivotal for various sides to understand one another whenever possible. For example, it's easy to assume the average born-again consumer's behavior comes from a position of bigotry or hate. This position is largely the result of the segment holding a different view on how thriving and flourishing are accomplished in people, and whether identity politics helps or harms those who are caught up in such initiatives. This segment is less interested in living in a news cycle while shopping for a pair of shoes. They'd prefer a break from the overt positioning and politicizing on key issues. So how do these views impact how you might market a product or service?

This segment is less interested in living in a news cycle while shopping for a pair of shoes. They'd prefer a break from the overt positioning and politicizing on key issues.

This data reveals the clear divergences in the worldviews of the population of our nation. Marketers are certainly able to highlight woke movements; they have been doing so. One does wonder, though, if such willingness will persist with the same intensity moving forward if companies begin to realize it could be costing them market share.

If brands are communicating from a position of legitimate conviction, there is no reason to believe their tactics will change. If such advertising has more to do with attempting to take the temperature of American culture in order to increase reach and profits, a shift in promotional strategies could be on the table.

In the ever-connected digital world, marketing leaders will be forced to vocationally consider these and other social issues and determine if they are helping or hurting their efforts. Other issues that see a significant divergence across the population include immigration, abortion, and climate change, all areas that conservative, religious consumers are less tolerant toward and that don't garner as much widespread support as perhaps advertisers assume they do.

ACTIVATION

This and the previous nine spiritugraphics have the potential to offer a new framework for the way advertisers approach this significant percentage of the American consumer population.

That's why our agency wanted to write this book. We have benefited from these insights for two decades. What would lead us to print our "secrets"? The simple fact of the matter is this: There are plenty to go around. This market and these insights are an abundant, largely untapped reality. Spiritugraphics is an entirely independent factor our industry has not weighed, in large part because these topics can be challenging to discuss.

The study validated much of what we've seen firsthand as advisors and brand builders. Together we can now recognize the importance of relationship and reputation to the connected, embedded, born-again shopper. We appreciate the power of the empty-nest household of faith. Christmas and "Made in America" are two silver bullets that cost nothing to press on further and will increase market share simply by mentioning. Untapped earnings are available at the same time each year during Lent if you pivot your focus. Daughters are different for most households—especially born-again homes—and they aren't mirroring cultural icons to the extent that many in the industry might assume. America is more conservative than our industry might realize, and the born-again home is willing to stand on principle, which could cost your brand in the end. Finally, born-again homes are more old-school and small-town than we usually represent within the industry. In short, these thirty-eight million households are a gold mine waiting to be engaged.

PART 3

Activating Spiritugraphics for Your Brand

CHAPTER 16

Implementing This New Framework

———

Here's where the work begins. It's one thing to read a book and ponder its insights, but it's another thing entirely to bring a brand into alignment with something new. Especially when the new thing can be boiled down to "We're going to harmonize our brand with the accents of the Christian-minded market so we can harvest their engagement more effectively."

There are economic and relational reasons to do this. You can get a bump with the most stable two-thirds of the US market without sacrificing anything about your brand. As you do this, you will gain not only new levels of customer loyalty and relationships but also messaging prerogatives and latitude you've never enjoyed before because you'll be orienting to more enduring and more inclusive truths than your previous choices. Your brand will become more stable, your messaging more consistent and more precise, and your culture far more durable than your status quo.

You will also deliver greater life value for your team. Here's what we mean by that. The management consulting

You can get a bump with the most stable two-thirds of the US market without sacrificing anything about your brand.

firm of McKinsey & Company coined an idea they call Meaning Quotient, or MQ. It's meant to live alongside Intelligence Quotient (IQ) and Emotional Intelligence Quotient (EQ). McKinsey found there are five types of meaning employees find most important in the work they do. The five are evenly distributed so each of the five is the most critical to 20 percent of your employees.

McKinsey has different names for the five categories, but like most marketing frameworks, we've translated these into the alliterative Five Cs of MQ:

1. *Career*. Personal rewards and successes. (Spiritugraphics clears the way to improved results and higher personal gratification.)
2. *Company*. The performance of the organization. (Spiritugraphics wins free ground, helps avoid costly short-term choices, and strengthens the brand platform.)
3. *Coworker*. How the team and culture perform together. (Spiritugraphics tables critical topics and invites long-view balances in perspective.)
4. *Customer*. The impact of the brand on the lives of customers. (Spiritugraphics helps you know how to win loyalty and show honor to your customers.)
5. *Community*. How the brand matters to the world. (Spiritugraphics opens all sorts of doors in

messaging and operations to align the brand with community interests.)

The more effectively you address all five *C*s every time you speak to your team, the greater your return on your organization's MQ.

No framework will help you clarify and codify your organization's MQ, and the sense of life meaning and work value your team experiences, like the intentional application of spiritugraphics. The discussions will be about your customer and about how you compete in the market, but you'll really be figuring out how your organization can live honestly and from places of affirmation in a time when teams are starved for meaning and connection. Spiritugraphics is a critical tool in doing the right thing for every constituent in all five *C*s of MQ.

Let's summarize why the application of a spiritugraphic layer is worth pursuing:

1. A market bump: increased wins and decreased losses across multiple consumer segments. And there are future gains for the lifetime value you create.
2. A leaner and more stable brand platform based on the consumer body, mind, and *heart*.
3. A stronger, more empowered, more durable team that is customer-centric.

Spiritugraphics is a whole new toolset arriving at the perfect cultural moment. It will help you identify drag in your current processes and refine your approach so you can go faster with greater efficiency.

CHAPTER 17

Now What, So What? A Primer on Activating Spiritugraphics

Today's marketer navigates an ever-changing land-scape to connect theory to application. Spiritugraphics is no different. It begins as a data-driven theoretical framework, but it also offers rich opportunities for activating this newfound consumer insight.

Here are a few steps to consider as you think about your brand and begin to map out a tactical plan of action for your marketing efforts. We suggest working through these questions while thinking about your brand, holding existing campaigns or messaging frameworks against the same light, and keeping your conversation broad and high-level for as long as you can before you transition into the real work of creating specific marketing expressions.

☐ Review the list of spiritugraphics and meanings from the previous chapters. Thinking of them as personality traits, which are the strongest for your brand as a natural extension of your existing efforts? Which are the weakest or feel the least relevant to your brand?

☐ Which of the spiritugraphics frustrate you the most? Why? (Sometimes this can reveal a space where biases are costing you and where a short-term frustration or some irrational need to "win" a messaging contest could be upgraded with a long-term perspective change.)

☐ Review the ways each spiritugraphic can dial up or down, and consider where your brand stands and where you might have opportunities for net gains.

☐ How far can you turn your brand's core and secondary dials without creating huge blowback tax internally or with your customers?

☐ Where might you be creating negative sentiment expenses for your brand based on your current creative, message, and activities?

☐ With this new filter, where do you think you might be spending money with nominal ROI trades (e.g., the readily available bump with little downside risk of "Christmas" versus "Lent")?

☐ Which would be easiest and which the most difficult to apply spiritugraphic direction: marketing, sales, product, operation, culture?

CHAPTER 18

Selling the Framework (Internally)

———

Continuing with the action steps, you may be contemplating how to introduce or gain buy-in for spirtugraphics from your team. As with any new idea, it's wise for the pioneer to be prepared for key conversations. This is especially true with the spiritugraphics framework because modern rules of engagement (not to mention human resources and public relations coaching) tend to steer us away from discussions of religion or politics. Doubly so when you're talking about engaging people's budgets and livelihoods.

First, have you ever heard of Rock Paper Scissors for business? It might be useful.

Instead of Rock Paper Scissors, in business it's called Power Moral High Ground Analytics. Power tends to focus on the past and competence, high moral ground on the future and meaning, and analytics on the present and performance. Moral high ground trumps power ("That's great that we're the best-trained police force in the country—are we making a difference?"), analytics trumps moral high ground

("That's great we're making a difference—is the approach sustainable?"), and power trumps analytics ("I see the data you're showing me—we're the best-trained police force in the country; if we can't figure it out, nobody can.").

Instead of Rock Paper Scissors, in business it's called Power Moral High Ground Analytics. Power tends to focus on the past and competence, moral high ground on the future and meaning, and analytics on the present and performance.

Think of the people you need to convince to give the spiritu-graphics framework a shot. Do you know immediately which people are going to flash you the rock of power, the scissors of moral high ground, or the paper of analytics?

If you're not sure, here's your one-question diagnostic, and you can ask it very casually: "What makes you optimistic about the future of the organization?" (If they're not optimistic, ask why and you'll get the same insight.) If they answer with past or competence, they're likely thinking in terms of power. If they answer with future and meaning, they're likely biased toward moral high ground. If they answer with the present and a data snap-shot of some sort, they're likely wired to be more agreeable to the analytics approach.

Steps for Gaining Traction with the Rock Paper Scissors Approach

1. Name the people you need to convince at an exec-utive level.

2. Which are power, which are moral high ground, and which are analytics?
3. What objections do you already anticipate from them? Ideally, you will find a reason or two from each of power, moral high ground, and analytics.
4. What's your best single-point argument for increased competence?
5. What's your best single-point argument for increased meaning?
6. What's your best single-point argument for increased performance?

Now you're ready to play. People tend not to worry a whole lot about the category they trump so be ready with a light "as you know" touch there as a reminder of the goad they experience from such people. People tend to fill their own sweet spot effectively, so offer a simple "as you would imagine" review of your best single-point argument on their sweet spot. Enough to give them a launching point for their own thinking. And then put the "and what's really cool" emphasis on the category that tends to trump them. People tend to need one point of departure to push off from what's behind them, one great starting point for their sweet spot, and one killer focus point to address what they're running into.

> *People tend to need one point of departure to push off from what's behind them, one great starting point for their sweet spot, and one killer focus point to address what they're running into.*

Do this, and you'll win the chance to look at your organization through the lens of the spiritugraphics framework with your peers and chart a path to fresh wins.

ACTION STEPS WITH PEERS
(BEFORE FULL TEAM ROLLOUT)

Not only are you introducing a new market filter to complement demographics, psychographics, and whatever other matrices you use, you're introducing a filter that's based in the charged realm of American spirituality. If you roll this into your processes well, you'll be a hero and you'll generate major new results. There's great demand for major new results, but few people on your team are likely to be waiting for you to show up with a bunch of thinking about how spiritual perspectives should drive corporate initiatives. It's important you test your thinking and win buy-in carefully. Here are our suggestions for introducing spiritugraphics to your peers or core team before you go broad with a less predictable internal audience.

1. *Review and compare notes on the questions you answered in the first set of action steps.* Expect to be surprised by just how countercultural and ill-advised the approach feels to people. For people of faith, it can feel like a cheat code or manipulative framework. To others, you may see fears of draconian rigidity or concerns about selling out. In the end, there is far less actual manipulation or cultural risk with spiritugraphics than there is with demographics or psychographics, but the more you test and discuss it, the surer your footing will be later.

2. *Do some rough cost-analysis work.* Start with current spending that feels like it's approaching diminished returns. Is there a ceiling with the market and consumer to which you're communicating? Bad campaigns are like meetings: there won't be resistance if they get canceled. Then look at where your brand might be paying a "tax" in the form of either offense or irrelevance (which should be what you find most offensive). What buyer behavior costs, competitor openings, and internal morale expenses can you estimate?

   Next, where do you see free money? Are there spaces where you can pull a lever with no tradeoffs for the brand and organization? These should not be related to your core spiritugraphic but could have a halo effect in both directions.

   Finally, do some loose assessments related to how you could leverage a primary and secondary spiritugraphic to amplify your current strengths. Do this with a conservative view of your gains and a pessimistic assumption about the tradeoffs you'll experience, because bad news comes faster and tends to sound louder than good news.

3. *Create a preliminary testing and primary spiritu-graphic go-to-market calendar* based on the previous cost-analysis work and the receptivity you antici-pate from your internal teams and outside vendors. Assume delays, rework, and a socially onerous process as support teams come into alignment. Use this conversation to make plans to uncover both broad value (spiritugraphics writ large) and specific

value (individual ardently progressive or irreligious stakeholders) for the organization.

4. *Determine objective filters, limits, or benchmarks* to help guide the subjective and creative conversations that will follow.

5. *Find expertise related to these faith insights.* Matters of the (consumer) heart can't be faked—it's critical to root any efforts with this segment in authentic understanding of what drives these buyers. This expertise may be found on your team or with an outside resource that lives and breathes this framework.

ENGAGING TEAMS

For some teams, spiritugraphics will be adopted as simple market data akin to demographics or psychographics. That's what it is.

For others, spiritugraphics will come across as catering to a portion of society that stands for outdated beliefs and sees the world through filters that are questioned in modern-day culture. Such views on the faith-based population are popularized, but that's not what the spiritugraphics framework is about.

For teams that feel a reluctance to embrace spiritugraphics, two points are worth discussing.

1. *Is the organization seeking success in the short term or in the long term?* Like most brand-building efforts, there's a discipline and time horizon. The organizations that will have the ongoing ability to steer

conversations and shape culture are the ones that understand it and win the audience through insight and the efficient use of loyalty-building processes. You can be reactive and loud now but small and irrelevant later, or you can be wise and consistent over time and articulate a better world all along the way.

2. *The best way to shape perceptions is to find meaningful common ground and influence the behavior of tribes.* The gap between tribes in today's world is not the result of both sides understanding each other and disagreeing; it's frustration and an increasingly shrill screaming right past each other in languages and paradigms that are foreign to the other. It is the job of the professional communicator to understand the audience and then translate for impact. Spiritugraphics is a unique tool for reclaiming voice and bridging unhealthy social gaps. It doesn't come from a place of judgment of a consumer market; rather, it's an opportunity to connect and engage with relevance.

> *The organizations that will have the ongoing ability to steer conversations and shape culture are the ones that understand it and win the audience through insight and the efficient use of loyalty-building processes.*

SUGGESTED ACTION STEPS WITH TEAMS

We're thinking of teams here as internal or external marketing, sales, support, product, or channel teams, as well as executive and financial teams with exposure to how a brand is managed and expressed. Here are steps to consider with your team(s):

1. *Review the initial perceptions and conclusions* from the previous peer conversations. Discuss and debate both the definitions and the conclusions.

2. *Review the cost-analysis work.* Make the business case for the framework. You'll want to consider the market size that's available, what it costs to reach it, and the associated lifetime value or brand lift from doing so. This is also where you can account for retaining your current base and welcome a new consumer group to your party.

3. *Review the testing and go-to-market calendars.* Focus especially on streamlining, anticipated efficiencies, and where you might benefit from an overlap communicating to multiple consumer segments at the same time.

4. *Capture a list of personal misgivings among the team,* especially as they relate to specific spiritugraphics or how specific choices on a spiritugraphics continuum feels like a threat or frustration to team members. This list will also serve as a litmus test for the comfort level your team has in activating a spiritugraphics insight.

5. *Discuss the misgivings* through the lens of "personal threat" and "brand threat." If, for example, the Old-School (body art) spiritugraphic creates a

sense of personal threat to artistic freedom, generational preferences and behaviors, or cultural
norms, that's a great misgiving to document and
bake into a creative and operational review process.
On the other hand, if the threat feels more like a
brand threat in the sense that covered up arm
sleeves in a Gap ad will be seen as less cutting
edge and therefore less successful in the market or
trade publications, that's a marker to test and follow
the data about. (Sometimes social agendas don't
line up with market dynamics, at which point an
organization should make informed decisions about
the cost they want to absorb for the social agenda.
This is true in both directions, obviously.)

CHAPTER 19

Creative Application for Your Brand

———

Eventually your spiritugraphics considerations need to be baked into your brand platform and playbook the same way as demographics, psychographics, and all your copy and design guidelines are. Here's one cadence for your consideration.

1. *Determine your dominant spiritugraphic,* the one that most closely harmonizes with the "soul" of your brand. Your brand's authenticity is nonnegotiable, and it'll be difficult to sustain any lift or gain if you're faking a spiritugraphic for a short-term gain.

2. *Determine where on that spiritugraphic's continuum you expect to find your sweet spot* in terms of your greatest net buyer-demonstrated value (positive response and downstream leverage, less negative reaction).

3. *Rewrite the definitions* of the insight, the meaning your audience ascribes to the insight, and the way you think about the continuum so the framework

becomes distinctly and usefully yours. It should echo your brand voice.

4. *Name and illustrate the "near miss" and "wild miss"* continuum expressions of your brand. You've seen this with logo treatment guidelines. Have fun and see if absurdity produces anything especially poignant for you.

5. *Repeat the first four steps with primary and tertiary spiritugraphics.* Think of this the way you would think of primary, secondary, and tertiary brand colors, and see if you find any amplified value in the way they harmonize.

6. *Explore the "free money" spiritugraphics* you identified previously but don't see as core for the brand. Do you see an obvious application path for them now? Is there a reason your brand team hasn't explored the "free money" actions before?

7. *Audit your existing brand expressions* within the spiritugraphic framework. Which spiritugraphics have been your dominant voice, and where on the continuum of each have you been spending your energy? What's the best stuff to cut? What's worth tweaking? What should you leave alone for now as you roll other materials into the mix? Applying one spiritugraphic well outweighs trying to integrate ten at once.

8. *Survey your primary competitors through the spiritugraphics lens.* Does your entire industry tend to gravitate toward specific postures? What's the competitive opportunity available to you? What positioning, messaging, and channels are they leaving on the table? Hint: they're probably not

using and benefiting from spiritugraphics for the same or similar reasons your team hasn't activated these insights.

9. *Consider your value proposition* and the way customers would summarize your brand in light of the way you're heading with spiritugraphics filters. Does anything need to be tweaked at a core level for marketing, sales, delivery, HR, or philanthropic expressions? Your honesty will also help curb any desire to release inauthentic attempts with this consumer segment.

10. *Build a few new personas based on what you're figuring out.* If you're realizing that your sweet spot is dialing up one spiritugraphic, you might look at a persona that matches directly but isn't all that impressed (the Baptist who goes to Chick-fil-A but doesn't think about why she feels so comfortable there), a dial-flat persona who's exceedingly impressed and grateful (the loosely church-affiliated person who is far more likely to evangelize for "the Lord's chicken" than for the Lord), and the dialed-down customer who's ready to hit social media with an angry story if he can find one. These personas can work in the opposite direction, too, if you think about the brand that uses the dialed down "Happy Holidays" but is met with a social media troll ready to remind the world that "Jesus is the reason for the season." As you know, personas take on a life of their own. The point is to consider creating the right number of spiritugraphically informed personas for your brand and the team supporting it.

11. *Determine your copy and design boundaries.* In nearly
    all cases, we can say things in far more explicit
    terms than we can show them before we pay a
    reaction tax. What are the right boundaries for
    tattoos and piercings for your audience? What
    about heavy makeup and revealing clothing for
    your preteen market? Create a list of phrases and
    image concepts that you've used before or that
    seem likely to come up in brand expressions going
    forward. Determine some sort of green, yellow, red
    approach to what works, what works sparingly, and
    what needs an alternative.

12. *Be aware of, and consider the filter guidance* offered by
    entities such as the Human Rights Campaign (HRC),
    which tracks corporate support of ESG concerns
    as well as public expressions of that support. The
    scoring and subsequent public relations pressure
    such entities can deliver is a legitimate business
    factor to consider. Some entities will push for
    more than what your brand might give, and others
    might grade in a fashion you can't afford to meet.
    But based on the huge percentage of corpora-
    tions receiving top marks from HRC in particular,
    "watchdog" groups are a decent complement to spir-
    itugraphics thinking and can be a great way to play
    to the largest market opportunity without doing so at
    the expense of minority audiences. You can't please
    everyone all of the time, but there's very rarely a
    good business case for offending anyone. And even
    when tribes seem to thrive on offending one another,

few tribes actually ascribe to that sort of behavior as an expression of their values. Professional communicators, especially marketers, should be masters of crafting winning messages where the only real costs are opportunity costs you incur as you maximize value for your brand.

13. *Execute with new success metrics in mind.* Bad news will come faster than good news, and will look scarier in its delivery. Categorize the bad news: what sort of feedback is it, really? All change will create a negative response from some portion of your audience who doesn't like change. Some feedback will be evidence that you're upsetting a norm of some sort, and that should be watched. Some will possibly generate press or protest, and that should have been expected and already "paid for" within your organization.

Professional communicators, especially marketers, should be masters of crafting winning messages where the only real costs are opportunity costs you incur as you maximize value for your brand.

The good news tends to arrive on at least a quarterly lag, in the form of trends and other indicators. You've already done the preliminary cost analysis. Now's the time to watch and see if you can track impact and results by the segments you're targeting.

14. *Don't be reactive.* Pursue the good thing that is true of your brand. Every expression sets an expectation so it needs to be authentic, sustained, and something you can rest in while the waves settle.

15. *Grow.* Continue to audit your efforts and assumptions. Survey your audience and see if there's a difference between the Methodist Mark and Presbyterian Paula personas. In the end, spiritugraphics is nothing more than a reflection of the hope and beauty your audience has chosen to care about with their dollars and behaviors. Done well, embracing spiritugraphics should be the thing that brings meaning and traction to your organization, helps you see around corners when your customers are ready for a new offering, and influences which version of you shows up at work and goes home to the ones you love.

CHAPTER 20

There Is So Much More to Explore Together

A s agency veterans, we believe that spiritugraphics is more than a theory. It's been part of our advisory work for nearly a quarter of a century (even if we didn't always have a moniker for it).

Sure, the research and findings help galvanize the hypothesis that a large segment of US consumers behave differently. And the data set has proven to be readily actionable. But perhaps the best measure is what we've experienced firsthand: there are real-life brands strategically winning in this market, and it's not by accident.

We've shared a few of these brands and case studies throughout, and we suspect you'll start decoding spiritugraphics all around you—next time you're ordering a cup of coffee, waiting for a flight, or cheering on your favorite sports team, you're likely to see spiritugraphics in play. They're all around us. Some are subtle, some are obvious. What's clear is that there's an addressable market waiting to hear from you. The question is, how will you dial your brand up or down to reach them?

We see a shared win in any instance where a brand can understand its customer better, reach them with more respect, and align offerings with what the customer values. Demographics identifies and helps marketers connect with customers more effectively, even if the categories of demography fail to probe deeply into a person. Psychographics reaches further, into the mindsets of people, to see their behaviors and meet them with solutions that are immediately compelling and convey new sources of value.

There's an addressable market waiting to hear from you. The question is, how will you dial your brand up or down to reach them?

With spiritugraphics, we believe your connection with your customer will grow even more profound at a heart level, and that this connection will produce even greater loyalty, perceived value, and collaboration between brands and customers. Spiritugraphics is a new way to do your job more effectively and to do it from a place of heart and humanity in an era where heart and humanity have never been more appreciated. The win accrues to anyone who will choose to note, appreciate, and engage the hearts of their customers. That means you and your customers or clients. It also means us and our ongoing desire to lead this conversation and open this way of addressing the marketplace.

You're not alone. As you adopt this new consumer framework, you'll have a community of peers implementing spiritugraphics with their brand teams. We'll continue to post content, findings, and resources at **Spiritugraphics.com**.

And if you need a hand, we'll be here to help you reach a wider and more loyal audience.

EXECUTIVE SUMMARY

PURPOSE

This study was a national study of women to examine how faith affects their buying and spending decisions. Specifically, this study investigated the following areas of concern:

- Where Do They Shop?
- What Is Important When They're Shopping?
- Are They Shopping Differently Today?
- How Does Their Faith Affect Their Shopping?

SPECIFIC POINTS

I. General Tendencies

1. **How does faith affect their life decisions?**

   Among those who would not get a tattoo, 29.2% said it is a faith-driven decision, and 26.4% of those who would not get a body piercing said it is a faith-driven decision.

2. **How does faith affect their buying decisions?**

   One-third (32.9%) of those surveyed said they

buy from Hobby Lobby because of their very public Christian faith. Forty-six percent (46.4%) said they prefer Chick-fil-A in part due to its Christian values as a company.

3. **What do they give up for Lent?**
Among those who change their diet during Lent by eating different foods than normal, 34.3% said they avoid meat.

4. **How does their faith affect where they buy?**
Sixty percent said they would not shop at a store if it sold pornographic books/videos. Forty-five percent said they would not shop at a store that hired illegal immigrants.

5. **Do they ever shop at a Christian bookstore?**
Twenty-five percent said they would go to a Christian bookstore if they were going to buy a Bible.

6. **Do they give Christian gifts such as Bibles?**
Thirty-three percent said they have given a Bible as a gift.

II. Public Service/Political Activity
What is their political philosophy?
Fifty-three percent said their political philosophy is conservative/very conservative, 21.7% said they are moderate, and 20.2% said they are liberal.

III. Entertainment Choices
1. **How much does faith influence which movies they watch?**

Fourteen percent said their faith "very much" influences the movies they see.

2. **Which TV channels do they watch?**
   Thirteen percent said their faith "very much" influences the TV shows they watch.

3. **Which TV channels do their children watch?**
   Sixteen percent said their faith "very much" influences the TV shows they let their children watch.

IV. Media versus Christians

1. **Do they believe social media influences teenagers?**
   Eighty-three percent said they feel social media has too much influence on teenagers.

2. **Do they believe social media influences women in their 20s?**
   Seventy percent said they feel social media has too much influence on women in their 20s.

V. Shopping Preferences

Do they notice which stores decorate for Christmas?
Twenty-nine percent said they are more likely to purchase a product using "Christmas" in the title.

PROCEDURE

The data obtained in this study was by telephone interviews of a qualified sample in the United States (N=1,000) with samples for: Pacific (N=160), North Central/ Mountain (N=138), East North Central (N=154), South Central (N=177), New England/Middle Atlantic (N=179), and South Atlantic (N=192). The qualified sample was selected by random digit procedure ensuring construction of a probability sample. A copy of the questionnaire used in this survey is included in this report. Detailed findings as well as computer cross-tabulations of the responses obtained to each question by selected demographic characteristics are also provided.

The survey began on December 11, 2020, and concluded on January 27, 2021.

KEY OBSERVATION FINDINGS

1. The Pacific sample consists of 160 qualified consumers in the following states. Alaska, California, Hawaii, Oregon, and Washington.
2. The North Central/Mountain sample consists of 138 qualified consumers in the following states: Arizona, Colorado, Idaho, Iowa, Kansas, Minnesota, Missouri, Montana, Nebraska, Nevada, New Mexico, North Dakota, South Dakota, Utah, and Wyoming.
3. The East North Central sample consists of 154 qualified consumers in the following states: Illinois, Indiana, Michigan, Ohio, and Wisconsin.
4. The South Central sample consists of 177 qualified consumers in the following states: Alabama, Arkansas, Kentucky, Louisiana, Mississippi, Oklahoma, Tennessee, and Texas.
5. The New England/Middle Atlantic sample consists of 179 qualified consumers in the following states: Connecticut, Maine, Massachusetts, New Hampshire, New Jersey, New York, Pennsylvania, Rhode Island, and Vermont.

6. The South Atlantic sample consists of 192 qualified consumers in the following states: Delaware, District of Columbia, Florida, Georgia, Maryland, North Carolina, South Carolina, Virginia, and West Virginia.

7. This is a qualified study of female consumers.

8. Two in five said "go to the store with the best selection" best fits them.

9. One in five said they grew up in South Central, consisting of Alabama, Arkansas, Kentucky, Louisiana, Mississippi, Oklahoma, Tennessee, and Texas.

10. Two in five said they don't know the population of the area where they grew up.

11. Of those who said they no longer live in an area with a population of 100,000 or less, three in ten said they wish they would have stayed there and not gone to a more populated community.

12. Five in nine said they prefer shopping in stores.

13. One in two said shopping in stores is fun for them.

14. Of those who said shopping in stores is not fun for them, one in four said "worried about COVID-19" is what makes it not fun today.

15. Over three in five said they try to buy from neighborhood/ locally owned retailers whenever they can.

16. One in four said they make a special effort to find out which stores are active in local community programs.

17. Of those who make a special effort to find out which stores are active in local community programs, over one in three said "know of their reputation" is how they find out about these retailers.

18. Two in five said they believe Walmart is a good active community retailer.

19. One in five said the reputation of the company/business they buy from is "very important."

20. Of those who said the reputation of the company/business they buy from is "very important," two in three said reputation is more important to them that the price of the item (but that's only 14% of the total population).

21. Three in five said they "can't recall" the last time they experienced an incredible customer service experience in a retail store.

22. One in seven said Walmart is the store where they experienced an incredible customer service experience.

23. One in eleven said "within the last 6 months" is the last time they experienced an incredible customer service experience online.

24. Two in five said Amazon is the website where they experienced an incredible customer service experience (but that's only 10% of the universe).

25. Over one in three said they are shopping at Walmart more compared to 3–5 years ago.

26. One in four said they are shopping at Target less compared to 3–5 years ago.

27. Four in nine said they are shopping at Amazon more compared to 3–5 years ago.

28. Three in ten said they are shopping at Wayfair/Overstock more compared to 3–5 years ago.

29. Over one in three said they are shopping at local neighborhood family-owned stores more compared to 3–5 years ago.

30. One in four said they are shopping at off-priced retailers such as Marshalls, TJ Maxx, and Ross less compared to 3–5 years ago.

31. Over one in four said they are shopping at smaller discount stores such as Family Dollar, Dollar General, and Fred's more compared to 3–5 years ago.

32. Over one in two said they are shopping at enclosed malls less compared to 3–5 years ago.

33. Three in ten said they are shopping at freestanding stores less compared to 3–5 years ago.

34. Five in nine said they or someone in their family shop at thrift stores.

35. Four in nine said they or someone in their family shop at consignment stores.

36. One in six said a busy active lifestyle "very much" makes shopping less fun because they have less time today.

37. Four in nine said shopping at stores just takes too much time today for them to do it very often.

38. One in five said "trying items on" is what they miss in a retail store experience by buying more online and less in the stores.

39. Three in five said they shop individually.

40. Over three in five said they are more likely to buy the store brand.

41. Four in nine said they think many store brands are nearly equal to name brands.

42. One in four said they think many store brands are equal to name brands.

43. Five in nine said they are a better quality buyer.

44. One in six said they are a best quality buyer.

45. One in four said they are a good quality buyer.

46. Two in three said they want professional salespeople in stores.

47. Over one in two said they will get the lowest prices in

a store.

48. Of those who feel they will get the lowest prices in a store, one in two said "stores have big sales" is why they believe the store will be lower priced.

49. Of those who feel they will get the lowest prices online, three in five said "more to choose from/better selection" is why they believe online will be lower priced.

50. Three in ten said they go online to find out the latest styles and fashions for their children.

51. One in three said they go online to find out the latest styles and fashions for themselves.

52. One in four said they typically spend $751–$1,000 on Christmas gifts per year.

53. Over one in five said they will spend $36–$50 on each gift this year.

54. Only three in ten said they are "more likely" to purchase a product using "Christmas" rather than "holiday" in their title during the Christmas shopping season.

55. Two in five said they would try to get approved for 0% interest and pay it off interest-free over time if they bought a computer or refrigerator.

56. Three in ten said "only spend what you can pay off" is their personal philosophy about using credit cards.

57. Two in five said someone in their family has been laid off, furloughed, or is working but less than before.

58. One in five said they would still shop at a store that sold pornographic books or videos.

59. Three in ten said they would still shop at a store that hired illegal immigrants.

60. About one in six said they are more likely to shop at Target due to its support of gay/lesbian rights.

61. About one in seven said they are more likely to shop at a store that is publicly in favor of Black Lives Matter.
62. Five in nine said they have watched more television over the last couple of months.
63. Of those who have watched more television over the last couple of months, over one in three said "news" is the type of programming they are watching more.
64. Seven in ten said they watch news on TV.
65. Of those who watch news on TV, over one in three said they watch Fox News most often.
66. Two in five said it bothers them when women wear short skirts, small bikinis, and lower necklines.
67. Nearly two in five said they don't worry about how short women's skirts are today.
68. Of those who worry about how short women's skirts are today, two in five said "just above the knee" is appropriate.
69. One in two said "2 buttons" is how many buttons should be unbuttoned for a blouse to be appropriate.
70. Over one in three said they shop at Victoria's Secret.
71. Three in four said they wear makeup whenever they go out.
72. One in four said they would spend over $500 for a necklace/earrings.
73. Of those who would spend over $500 for a necklace/earrings, one in six said Tiffany is their favorite jewelry brand.
74. One in seven said they would spend over $500 for a watch.
75. Of those who would spend over $500 for a watch, one in six said Rolex is their favorite watch brand.

76. Two in five said they have considered getting a tattoo.
77. Of those who have not considered getting a tattoo, three in ten said it's a faith-driven decision.
78. Two in five said they have considered getting a body piercing.
79. Of those who have not considered getting a body piercing, one in four said it's a faith-driven decision.
80. Four in five said they will go to an R-rated movie.
81. Two in five said they or someone in their family is a Harry Potter fan.
82. Three in ten said they had read *Fifty Shades of Grey*.
83. One in four said they think their family's greatest financial challenge this year is "unexpected bills like car repairs."
84. One in three said they have two credit cards.
85. One in eight said "feel a lot of pressure from bills and credit card debt" to describe their family's current debt level.
86. Of those who describe their family's current debt level as "feel some/a lot of pressure from bills and credit card debt," over one in two said that has been an issue for a number of years.
87. Two in five said "only buy essentials" is where they would cut back if they needed to reduce their monthly bills.
88. Only one in five said they care "very much" if something they wanted to buy is made somewhere out of the country.
89. Over one in five said "go online" or "wouldn't try to find out" is how they would find out which retailers/businesses were Christian-owned.
90. Two in five could not name a Christian-owned company.

91. Two in five first mentioned Chick-fil-A as a Christian-owned company.
92. Chick-fil-A had a combined response of 48.3 percent.
93. Hobby Lobby had a combined response of 32.2 percent.
94. Three in five said there is a Hobby Lobby where they live.
95. Of those who said there is a Hobby Lobby where they live, one in three said they buy from them because of their very public Christian faith.
96. Four in nine said they prefer Chick-fil-A in part due to its Christian values as a company.
97. Over four in five said they feel social media has too much influence on teenagers.
98. Seven in ten said they feel social media has too much influence on women in their 20s.
99. One in six said they feel social media has too much influence on them.
100. Three in four said they consider themselves to be a person of faith.
101. Of those who consider themselves to be a person of faith, five in nine said their faith has not affected what they buy or don't buy.
102. Two in three said they attend religious services.
103. Over three in four of those who attend a religious service said they dress differently to attend services.
104. Of those who dress differently to attend religious services, one in three said "nice dress" is how they dress differently.
105. Over one in five said "help others" is a characteristic a person of faith would exhibit.
106. Under two in five said they had a transformational experience by accepting Christ as their Savior.

107. Two in three said they go to church today.
108. One in five said they go to church once a week.
109. Three in ten said they would purchase a Bible from a bookstore.
110. One in seven said they change their diet by eating different foods than normal during Lent.
111. Of those who change their diet by eating different foods than normal during Lent, one in three said they avoid eating meat.
112. Three in five said they drink.
113. One in ten said "against my religion" is why they do not drink.
114. One in seven said faith "very much" influences where they go with their friends.
115. One in seven said faith "very much" influences the movies they see.
116. One in eight said faith "very much" influences the TV shows they watch.
117. One in six said faith "very much" influences the TV shows they let their children watch.
118. One in seven said faith "very much" influences the friends their children can go out with.
119. One in eight said faith "very much" influences the extra-school activities they will let their children participate in.
120. One in eight said faith "very much" influences the activities they take their family to.
121. Nearly two in five said "support it completely" as their opinion about gay marriage.
122. One in three said they have given a Bible as a gift.
123. One in seven said their political philosophy is "very conservative."

124. Three in ten said they shop most for everyday basic clothing at a department store.

125. Three in ten said they shop most for professional clothing online.

126. Three in five of those with children said their child did/does attend day care.

127. Of those with children who attend day care, one in five said it is a faith-centered day care program.

128. Over seven in ten of those with children said their child did/does attend a public school.

129. Two in five of those with children said they take an active role in the classes their child takes or in the teachers they will get in certain classes.

130. Of those who take an active role in the classes their child takes or in the teachers they will get in certain classes, virtually everyone said they take an active role in both the teachers they will get and certain classes.

131. One in two of those with children said they have both boys and girls.

132. One in two of those with girls said "fingertip" is the appropriate length of dress for her.

133. Over one in three of those with girls said a "one-piece" is what they consider to be an appropriate swimsuit for her.

134. One in seven of those with girls said they will allow their daughter to buy very short shorts.

135. Three in five of those with girls said they have told their daughter what they will accept it if she wants to buy a bikini.

136. Three in four of those with girls said there are a lot of clothing styles that are not acceptable for their daughter

to wear.

137. Five in six of those with girls said they restricted their younger daughters from certain items such as tight jeans, skimpy swimsuits, short shorts, or thigh-high skirts.

138. Of those with girls who said they restricted their younger daughters from certain items such as tight jeans, skimpy swimsuits, short shorts, or thigh-high skirts, one in four said their decision was based upon faith concerns.

139. Two in three of those with girls said they have told their girls they could not buy an item of clothing because it shows too much.

140. Of those with girls who said they have told their girls they could not buy an item of clothing because it shows too much, three in ten said a "skirt" was the item that revealed too much.

141. Seven in eight of those with children said there is a limit to how much they will allow their children to spend on name-brand athletic shoes.

142. Over three in five of those with children said they check the amount of time their children are on their cellphones/tablets.

143. Seven in ten of those with children said they check the websites their children are using.

144. Two in three said they are pro-life.

145. Two in five said "caused by humans" is their opinion related to climate change.

146. One in three said the "economy" is the issue that most influences their voting preferences.

147. Three in four said they believe God created the world.

148. One in four said they typically give none of their annual income to charity.
149. One in six said they typically give 9–10 percent of their annual income to charity.

TELEPHONE QUESTIONNAIRE

———

TELEPHONE NUMBER: _____

TIME BEGAN: _____

Hello, I'm _____ of Consumer Behavior Research Institute, a national research firm. We're talking to people in the United States today for this privately funded national study and your responses will be confidential.

A. Gender?

Male...18

Female...19

****IF "MALE," ASK FOR FEMALE IN HOUSEHOLD IF NONE, THANK AND TERMINATE****

---

1. Generally, which one would you say best fits you? **(READ LIST)**

Go to the lowest-priced store...495

Go to the store with the best selection...496

Go to the store that makes shopping easy and

takes care of its customers... 497

Go to a store selling the highest-quality merchandise...498

2. Where did you grow up?

Pacific...499	Alaska, California, Hawaii, Oregon, or Washington
North Central/ Mountain...500	Arizona, Colorado, Idaho, Iowa, Kansas, Minnesota, Missouri, Montana, Nebraska, Nevada, New Mexico, North Dakota, South Dakota, Utah, or Wyoming
East North Central...501	Illinois, Indiana, Michigan, Ohio, or Wisconsin
South Central...502	Alabama, Arkansas, Kentucky, Louisiana, Mississippi, Oklahoma, Tennessee, or Texas
New England/ Middle Atlantic...503	Connecticut, Maine, Massachusetts, New Hampshire, New Jersey, New York, Pennsylvania, Rhode Island, or Vermont
South Atlantic...504	Delaware, District of Columbia, Florida, Georgia, Maryland, North Carolina, South Carolina, Virginia, or West Virginia

---

3. What was the population of that area?

50,000 or less...505

50,001–100,000...506

100,001–500,000...507

500,001–1,000,000...508

Over 1 million ...509

(DON'T READ—Don't know...3)

---

4. IF "50,000 OR LESS" OR "50,001–100,000," ASK: Do you still live in that area?

IF "NO," ASK: Do you wish at times you would have stayed there and not moved to a more populated community?

Yes...1

No/Yes...604

No/No...605

Did not move to a more populated area...832

5. **Which do you prefer: shopping in-store or online?**

In-store... 510

Online...511

6. **Is shopping in stores fun for you?**

Yes...1

No...2

Don't know...3

7. **IF "NO," ASK: What makes it not fun today? (DON'T READ LIST)**

Checkout lines too long...512

Don't have enough money to spend...513

Don't have enough time...514

Dressing rooms closed...515

Have to wear a mask...516

No one available to help...517

Nothing new/unique...518

Prices too high/no good sales...519

Salespeople too pushy...520

Stores too crowded ...521

Worried about COVID-19...522

Other: _____

8. **Whenever you can, do you try to buy from neighborhood/locally owned retailers?**

Yes...1

No...2

Don't know...3

9. **Do you make a special effort to find out which stores are active in local community programs?**

Yes...1

No...2

Don't know...3

10. **IF "YES," ASK: How do you find out about these retailers? (DON'T READ LIST)**

Active in church...523

Ask friends/relatives...524

Go online...525
Know of their reputation...526
See advertising for them...527
Other: _____

---

11. Do you believe Walmart is a good active community retailer?

Yes...1
No...2
Don't know...3

---

12. How important is the reputation of the company/business you buy from?   **(READ LIST)**

Very important ...6
Somewhat important ...7
Not important ...9

---

13. IF "VERY IMPORTANT," ASK: Is reputation more important to you than the price of an item?

Yes...1
No...2
Don't know...3

---

14. When was the last time you experienced incredible customer service in a retail store?

Within the last 6 months...528
6 months–1 year ago...529
1–2 years ago...530
2–3 years ago...531

4–5 years ago...532
Over 5 years ago...533
(DON'T READ–Can't recall...215)

---

15. Which store was that?

(WRITE SPECIFIC STORE NAME)

16. When was the last time you experienced incredible customer service online?

Within the last 6 months... 528

6 months–1 year ago... 529

1–2 years ago...530

2–3 years ago...531

4–5 years ago...532

Over 5 years ago...533

(DON'T READ–Can't recall...215)

17. Which website was that?

(WRITE SPECIFIC WEBSITE NAME)

18. Compared to 3–5 years ago, are you shopping at Walmart more or less?

More...277

Less...263

(DON'T READ–Same...311)

19. Compared to 3–5 years ago, are you shopping at Target more or less?

More...277

Less...263

(DON'T READ–Same...311)

20. Compared to 3–5 years ago, are you shopping on Amazon more or less?

More...277

Less...263

(DON'T READ–Same...311)

21. Compared to 3–5 years ago, are you shopping on Wayfair/ Overstock more or less?

> More...277
>
> Less...263
>
> **(DON'T READ–Same...311)**

22. Compared to 3–5 years ago, are you shopping at local neighborhood family-owned stores more or less?

> More...277
>
> Less...263
>
> **(DON'T READ–Same...311)**

23. Compared to 3–5 years ago, are you shopping at off-price retailers such as Marshalls, TJ Maxx, and Ross more or less?

> More...277
>
> Less...263
>
> **(DON'T READ–Same..311)**

24. Compared to 3–5 years ago, are you shopping at smaller discount stores such as Family Dollar, Dollar General, and Fred's more or less?

> More... 277
>
> Less... 263
>
> **(DON'T READ–Same...311)**

25. Compared to 3–5 years ago, are you shopping at enclosed malls more or less?

> More...277
>
> Less...263
>
> **(DON'T READ–Same...311)**

26. Compared to 3-5 years ago, are you shopping at freestanding stores more or less?

More...277
Less...263
(DON'T READ—Same...311)

27. Do you or does anyone in your family shop at thrift stores?

Yes...1
No...2
Don't know...3

28. Do you or does anyone in your family shop at consignment stores?

Yes...1
No...2
Don't know...3

29. How much does a busy active lifestyle make shopping less fun because you have less time today? **(READ LIST)**

Very much... 534
Some,..535
Little/none,.,536

30. Does shopping at stores just take too much time today for you to do it very often?

Yes...1
No...2
Don't know...3

31. What do you miss from a retail store experience by buying more online and less in-store? **(DON'T READ LIST)**

Comparing side-by-side before buying...537
Getting information ...538
Making it an outing/event...539
Seeing quality/color...540
Taking things back there...541

Talking to salespeople...542

Trying items on...543

Working with people in

general...544

Other: _____

---

32. Do you shop as a family or do most family members pretty much go alone or with friends?

Shop as a family...833

Mainly shop individually...834

Don't know...3

---

33. When you shop at stores, are you more likely to buy the store brand to save money or buy the brand-name product because you trust the quality of the name brand?

Store brand...545

Name brand...546

---

34. Do you think many store brands are equal to or nearly equal to name brands?

Equal to...547

Nearly equal to...548

No... 2

---

35. Would you describe yourself today as a good-, better-, or best-quality buyer?

Good...15

Better...549

Best...550

---

36. When you buy in stores that have professional salespeople, do you like for them to be available when you want new information, or do you care if there are any professional salespeople working there?

Want professional salespeople...551

Don't care if there are professional salespeople...552

37. Where do you feel you will get the lowest prices in a store
or online?

> In-store...510
> Online...511

38. **IF "IN STORE," ASK:** Why do you believe the store will be lower
priced?   **(DON'T READ LIST)**

> Compared them to online companies...553
> Get special offers in the mail...554
> See ads in the newspaper...555
> See their ads on TV...556
> Stores have big sales...557
> Other : _____

39. **IF "ONLINE" TO #37, ASK:** Why do you believe online will be
lower priced?   **(DON'T READ LIST)**

> Direct to consumer...558
> Fewer employees...559
> Lower overhead...560
> More to choose from/better selection...561
> No expensive advertising...562
> Other : _____

40. Where do you go to find out the latest styles and fashions for
your children?

> Department stores...563
> Discount stores...564
> Local retailers...565
> Off-price retailers...566
> Online...511
> Specialty clothing stores...567
> Thrift stores...835
> Other: _____

41. Where do you go to find out the latest styles and fashions for yourself?

Department stores...563

Discount stores...564

Local retailers...565

Off-price retailers...566

Online...511

Specialty clothing stores...567

Thrift stores...835

Other : _____

42. Christmas is just around the comer; how much do you typically spend on Christmas gifts per year?

Nothing...93

$100 or less...568

$101–$250...569

$251–$350...570

$351–$500...571

$501–$750...572

$751–$1,000...573

$1,001–$2,500...574

Over $2,500...575

43. What will you spend on each gift this year?

$10 or less...576

$11–$15...577

$16–$20...578

$21–$25...579

$26–$35...580

$36–$50...581

$51–$75...582

$76–$100...583

Over $100...584

44. During the Christmas shopping season when you see some items using the word "Christmas" and others using the word "holiday" in the product title, are you more likely to purchase the product using "Christmas" in the title?

More likely...585

Less likely...586

No effect...836

45. If you bought a computer or refrigerator, would you try to get approved for 0% interest and pay it off interest-free over time?

Yes...1
No...2
Don't know...3

46. What is your personal philosophy about using credit cards?

Buy with credit card, pay with tax refund/bonus...587
Don't use them...588
Only spend what you can pay off...589
Use for big ticket items...590
Use for emergencies ...591
Use them to get a deal...592
Other: _____

47. Has anyone in your family been laid off, furloughed, or is working but less than before?

Yes...1
No...2
Don't know...3

48. If you knew a store sold pornographic books or videos, would you still shop there?

Yes...1
No...2
Don't know...3

49. If you learned a store had hired illegal immigrants, would you still shop there?

Yes...1
No...2
Don't know...3

50. Target has been a high-profile retailer supporting lesbian/
    gay rights: are you more or less likely to shop there due to its
    support of gay/lesbian rights?

                                                      More...277
                                                      Less...263
                                        (DON'T READ–Same...311)

51. A number of retailers have come out publicly in support of Black
    Lives Matter: are you more or less likely to shop at these stores?
                                                      More...277
                                                      Less...263
                                        (DON'T READ–Same...311)

52. Over these last couple of months, have you or your family
    watched more television?

                                                      Yes...1
                                                      No...2
                                                      Don't know...3

53. **IF "YES," ASK:** What type programming are you watching more?

Cartoons...593	Medical...601
Comedies...594	Movies...602
Cooking/food...595	News ...603
Crime...596	Political...838
Documentaries...837	Reality...604
Drama...597	Sitcoms...605
Family...598	Sports...606
Game shows...599	SyFy...607
Home-improvement/	Weather...608
homes...600	Other: _____

54. **Do you watch the news on TV?**

                                                      Yes...1
                                                      No...2
                                                      Don't know...3

55. IF "YES," ASK: Which network do you watch most often?

ABC...609   Fox News...614

CBS...610   MSNBC...615

CNBC...611   NBC...616

CNN...612   Don't know...3

FOX...613   Other: _____

---

56. Does it bother you when women wear short skirts, small bikinis, and lower necklines?

Yes...1

No...2

Don't know...3

---

57. Do you worry how short women's skirts are today? **IF "YES," ASK:** What is appropriate?

Yes/below the knee...617

Yes/just above the knee...618

Yes/mid-thigh...619

Yes/even shorter...620

No...2

---

58. How many buttons should be unbuttoned for a blouse to be appropriate?

1 button unbuttoned...621

2 buttons unbuttoned...622

3 buttons unbuttoned...623

4 buttons unbuttoned...624

---

59. Do you shop at Victoria's Secret?

Yes...1

No...2

Don't know...3

60. Do you wear makeup whenever you go out?

Yes...1

No...2

Don't know...3

61. Would you spend over $500 for a necklace/earrings?

Yes...1

No...2

Don't know...3

62. IF "YES," ASK: What is your favorite jewelry brand?

Cartier...636

Chanel ...637

David Yurman...638

Edward Mirell...639

Emmy London...640

Figaro...641

Gorjana...642

Gucci...643

Harry Winston...644

John Hardy...645

Kendra Scott...646

Le Vian...647

Marahlago Larimar...648

Mejuri...649

Neil Lane...650

Roberto Coin...651

The Last Line...652

Tiffany...653

Don't know...3

Other: _____

63. Would you spend over $500 for a watch?

Yes...1

No...2

Don't know...3

64. IF "YES," ASK: What is your favorite watch brand?

Cartier...636

Chanel...637

Citizen...654

David Yurman...638

Edward Mirell...639

Gucci...643

Harry Winston...644

Movado...655

OMEGA...656

Philip Stein...657

Rado...658
Rolex...659
TAG Heuer...660
Tiffany...653
Tissot...661

TUDOR...662
Victorinox...663
Don't know...3
Other: _____

---

65. Would you ever consider getting a tattoo? **IF "NO," ASK:** Is that a faith-driven decision?

Yes...1
No/yes...664
No/no... 665
Don't know...3

---

66. Would you ever consider a body piercing? **IF "NO," ASK:** Is that a faith-driven decision?

Yes...1
No/yes...664
No/no... 665
Don't know...3

---

67. Will you personally go to an R-rated movie?

Yes...1
No...2
Don't know...3

---

68. Are you or is anyone in your family a Harry Potter fan?

Yes...1
No...2
Don't know...3

---

69. Did you read *Fifty Shades of Grey*?

Yes...l
No...2
Don't know...3

70. What do you think is your family's greatest financial challenge
    this year?   (DON'T READ LIST)

    Car loans...666   Less income/no bonus...671
    College debt...667   Mortgage/rent... 839
    Credit card debt...668   Unexpected bills like car
    Finding a job...669   repairs...672
    Home repairs...670   Other: _____

71. How many credit cards do you have?

    None...4   Four...448
    One...445   Five...449
    Two...446   Over five...450
    Three...447

72. How would you describe your family's current debt level?
    (READ LIST)

              Feel no pressure at all from bills and credit card debt...673
              Feel some pressure from bills and credit card debt...674
              Feel a lot of pressure from bills and credit card debt...675

73. IF "FEEL SOME PRESSURE FROM BILLS AND CREDIT CARD
    DEBT" OR "FEEL A LOT OF PRESSURE FROM BILLS AND
    CREDIT CARD DEBT," ASK: Is that a new problem or one that
    has been an issue for a number of years?

                                        New problem...676
                                        For a number of years...677

74. Where would you cut back if you needed to reduce your monthly
    bills? (DON'T READ LIST)

                   Buy more store brands/less-expensive groceries...678
                                        Cable TV...679
                                        Cell phone contract...680
                                        Give less to charities...681
                                        Not go out to eat...682

Only buy essentials ...683

Other: _____

---

75. **How much do you care if something you want to buy is made somewhere out of the country?** **(READ LIST)**

Very much...534

Some...535

Little/none...536

---

76. **If you wanted to find out which retailers/businesses were Christian-owned, how would you go about finding out? (DON'T READ LIST)**

Ask friends/relatives...524

Ask pastor/people at church...684

Go online...525

Go to store website...685

Wouldn't try to find out...686

Other: _____

Can you name any stores that are Christian-owned?

77. **FIRST MENTION (DON'T READ LIST)**

Chick-fil-A...687	Wegmans...692
COOK OUT...688	Whole Foods...693
Forever 21...689	No...2
Hobby Lobby...690	Other: _____
In-N-Out...691	

---

78. **SECOND MENTION (DON'T READ LIST)**

Chick-fil-A687	Wegmans...692
Cook Out...688	Whole Foods...693
Forever 21...689	No...2
Hobby Lobby...690	Other: _____
In-N-Out...691	

79. Is there a Hobby Lobby near where you live? **IF "YES," ASK:** Hobby Lobby is a high-profile Christian retailer—do you buy from them because of their very public Christian faith?

Yes/yes...472
Yes/no...471
No...2
Don't know...3

80. Do you prefer Chick-fil-A in part due to its Christian values as a company?

Yes...1
No...2
Don't know...3

81. Do you feel social media has too much influence on teenagers?

Yes...1
No...2
Don't know...3

82. Do you feel social media has too much influence on women in their 20s?

Yes...1
No...2
Don't know...3

83. Do you feel social media has too much influence on you?

Yes...1
No...2
Don't know...3

84. Do you consider yourself a person of faith?

Yes...1
No...2
Don't know...3

85. IF "YES," ASK: In your opinion, how has faith affected what you buy or don't buy? **(DON'T READ LIST)**

Buy from places that give back to community...694

Live a simple life/not extravagant...695

Purchase modest clothing...696

Shop at companies with conservative values...697

Try to buy from local companies...698

It hasn't...699

Other: _____

---

86. How often do you attend religious services?

More than once a week...700

Once a week...248

Three times a month...701

Twice a month...702

Once a month...703

Less than once a month...704

Only on holidays...705

Never...10

---

87. IF ATTENDS, ASK: Do you dress differently to attend services? IF "YES," ASK: In what way do you dress differently? (DON'T READ LIST)

Hat...706

Heels...707

More conservative ...708

Nice dress...709

Nicer shirt/blouse...840

No jeans...710

No...2

Other: _____

---

88. What characteristics would a person of faith exhibit? (DON'T READ LIST)

Be gentle...711

Be kind...712

Generous...841

Help others...713

Humble/no brag...714

Not judgmental...715

Not raise voice/stay calm...716

Not swear...717

Pray...718

Other: _____

89. Did you have a transformational experience by accepting Christ as your savior?

Yes...1

No...2

Don't know...3

90. Which denomination do you go to today?

American Baptist Church...719

Assembly of God...720

Baptist...721

Bible Church...722

Catholic...723

Christian and Missionary
Alliance...724

Christian Church...725

Christian Science...726

Church of Christ...727

Church of God...728

Community Church...729

Episcopal (Anglican)...730

Evangelical Free Church...731

Jewish...732

Lutheran...733

Methodist...734

Mormon (Latter-Day
Saints)...735

Muslim...736

Nondenominational...737

Pentecostal...738

Presbyterian Church...739

None...4

Other: _____

91. How often do you go to church?

More than once a week...700

Once a week...248

Three times a month...701

Twice a month...702

Once a month...703

Less than once a month...704

Only on holidays ... 705

Never...10

92. If you were going to buy a Bible, where would you purchase it?

Bookstore...740

Christian bookstore...741

Discount store...742

Online...511

Other: _____

93. **During Lent, do you change your diet by eating different foods than normal?**

Yes...1
No...2
Don't know...3

94. **IF "YES," ASK: What foods do you avoid?**

Alcohol/beer ...751
Caffeine ...752
Candy/chocolate...844
Fast food...845

Meat...846
Sugar...847
Other: _____

95. **Do you drink? IF "NO," ASK: Why do you not drink?**

Afraid I can't stop...743
Against my religion...744
Going to AA/previous
    problem...745
Make poor choices...746
Never liked the taste...747

Not healthy...748
Sets bad example ...749
Too expensive... 750
Yes...1
Other: _____

Off the top of your head, how much does faith influence:

96. **Where you go with your friends? (READ LIST)**

Very much...534
Some...535
Little/none...536

97. **Which movies you see? (READ LIST)**

Very much...534
Some...535
Little/none...536

98. Which TV shows you watch? (READ LIST)

Very much...534

Some...535

Little/none...536

99. Which TV shows you let your children watch? (READ LIST)

Very much...534

Some...535

Little/none...536

100. Which friends your children can go out with? (READ LIST)

Very much...534

Some...535

Little/none...536

**101. Which extra-school activities you will let your children partici-
pate in? (READ LIST)**

Very much...534

Some...535

Little/none...536

102. What activities you would take your family to? (READ LIST)

Very much...534

Some...535

Little/none...536

103. What is your opinion related to gay marriage? (READ LIST)

Support it completely...753

Don't believe it is equal to traditional marriage...754

It is wrong...755

(DON'T READ–Don't know...3)

---

104. Have you ever given a Bible as a gift?

Yes...1

No...2

Don't know...3

---

105. How would you describe your political philosophy?
(READ LIST)

Very conservative...756

Conservative...757

Moderate...758

Liberal...759

Very liberal...760

---

106. Where do you shop most for everyday basic clothing: slacks,
pants, shirts, tops, and sweaters?

Ann Taylor...761

Department stores...762

Factory warehouse stores...763

High-end department
stores...764

Kohl's ... 765

Loft...766

Off-price retailers...767

Online...511

Specialty stores...768

Talbots ...769

Target...770

Walmart...771

Other: _____

---

107. Where do you shop most for nicer professional clothing such as
dresses, cashmere sweaters, business suits, and evening wear?

Ann Taylor...761

Department stores ...762

Factory warehouse stores...763

High-end department
stores...764

Kohl's ...765

Loft...766

Off-price retailers...767

Online...511

Specialty stores...768

Talbots...769

Walmart ...771

Target...770

Other: _____

Just a few statistical questions and we'll be through.

108. I'm going to read a list of age groups. Please stop me when I get to yours. (READ LIST)

Under 25...36

25–34...37

35–44...38

45–54...39

55–64...40

65 and over...41

109. What is the last grade of school you have completed? (READ LIST)

Less than high school...48

High school graduate...49

Some college...50

College graduate...51

Graduate school...52

110. What is your family status? (READ LIST)

Single...20

Single/children...21

Married...22

Married/children...23

Married/children away...24

111. IF "SINGLE/CHILDREN" OR "MARRIED/CHILDREN," ASK: Do your/did your children attend day care?

Yes...1

No...2

Don't know...3

112. **IF "YES," ASK:** Is that a faith-centered day care program?

Yes...1

No...2

Don't know...3

113. **IF "SINGLE/CHILDREN" OR "MARRIED/CHILDREN" TO #110,**
ASK: What type school does your child attend?

Public school...772

Christian school...773

Charter school...774

Homeschool...775

Catholic/parochial school...776

114. **IF "SINGLE/CHILDREN" OR "MARRIED/CHILDREN" TO #110,**
ASK: Do you take an active role in the classes your child takes
or in the teachers they will get in certain classes?

Yes/classes...777

Yes/teachers...778

Yes/both...354

No...2

115. **IF "SINGLE/CHILDREN" OR "MARRIED/CHILDREN" TO #110,**
ASK: Are your children boys or girls?

Boys...779

Girls...780

Both...213

116. **IF "GIRLS" OR "BOTH," ASK:** What is the appropriate length of
dress for her?

Mid-thigh ...781

Fingertip ...782

At the knee...783

Below the knee...784

Other: _____

117. **IF "GIRLS" OR "BOTH" TO #115, ASK:** What do you consider to
be an appropriate swimsuit for her?

Modest one-piece...785   Tankini...842

One-piece...786   Thong...790

Two-piece...787   Shirt/shorts...843

Bikini...788   Other: _____

String bikini...789

118. **IF "GIRLS" OR "BOTH" TO #115, ASK:** Shorts keep getting
shorter and shorter. Will you allow your daughter to buy these
very short shorts?

Yes...1

No...2

Don't know...3

119. **IF "GIRLS" OR "BOTH" TO #115, ASK:** Have you told your
daughter what you will accept if she wants to buy a bikini?

Yes...1

No...2

Don't know...3

120. **IF "GIRLS" OR "BOTH" TO #115, ASK:** Are there a lot of
clothing styles that are not acceptable for your daughter
to wear?

Yes...1

No...2

Don't know...3

121. **IF "GIRLS" OR "BOTH" TO #115, ASK:** When your daughter(s)
were little, did you restrict them from certain items such as tight
jeans, skimpy swimsuits, short shorts, or thigh-high skirts?
IF "YES," ASK: Was your decision based upon faith concerns?

Yes/yes ...472

Yes/no...471

No...2

122. **IF "GIRLS" OR "BOTH" TO #115, ASK:** Have you ever told one of your girls they could not buy an item of clothing because it shows too much?

Yes...1
No...2
Don't know...3

123. **IF "YES," ASK:** What was the garment you said revealed too much?

Crop top...791   Swimsuit...795
Low-neck top...792   Tight jeans...796
Short shorts...793   Other: _____
Skirt...794

124. **IF "SINGLE/CHILDREN" OR "MARRIED/CHILDREN" TO #110, ASK:** Is there a limit on how much you will allow your children to spend on name-brand athletic shoes?

Yes...1
No...2
Don't know...3

125. **IF "SINGLE/CHILDREN" OR "MARRIED/CHILDREN" TO #110, ASK:** Do you ever check the amount of time your children are on their cell phones/tablets?

Yes...I
No...2
Don't know...3

126. **IF "SINGLE/CHILDREN" OR "MARRIED/CHILDREN" TO #110, ASK:** Do you ever check the websites your children are visiting?

Yes...1
No...2
Don't know...3

127. Are you pro-life or pro-choice?

Pro-life...797

Pro-choice...798

128. What is your opinion related to climate change?

Caused by humans...799

Caused by nature...800

Don't believe it...801

Liberal idea...802

Not biblical...803

Other: _____

129. What issue most influences your voting preferences?

Abortion...804

Climate change...805

Coronavirus outbreak...806

Economic inequality...807

Economy ...808

Foreign policy...809

Gun policy...810

Health care...811

Immigration ...812

Race & ethnic inequality...813

Supreme Court
appointments...814

Violent crimes...815

Other: _____

130. Do you believe God created the world or that we evolved?

Created...816

Evolved...817

131. Now I'm going to read a list of combined income groups. Please stop me when I get to yours. **(READ LIST)**

Under $35,000...818

$35,000 to $54,999...819

$55,000 to $74,999...820

$75,000 to $99,999...821

$100,000 to $149,999...822

$150,000 and up...823

132. What percentage of your annual income do you typically give to charity?

None...4

9%–10%...828

1%–2%...824

11%–15%...829

3%–4%...825

16%–20%...830

5%–6%...826

More than 20%...831

7%–8%...827

133. Location? YOU MUST WRITE IN ZIP CODE

Pacific...499	Alaska, California, Hawaii, Oregon, or Washington
North Central/ Mountain...500	Arizona, Colorado, Idaho, Iowa, Kansas, Minnesota, Missouri, Montana, Nebraska, Nevada, New Mexico, North Dakota, South Dakota, Utah, or Wyoming
East North Central...501	Illinois, Indiana, Michigan, Ohio, or Wisconsin
South Central...502	Alabama, Arkansas, Kentucky, Louisiana, Mississippi, Oklahoma, Tennessee, or Texas
New England/ Middle Atlantic...503	Connecticut, Maine, Massachusetts, New Hampshire, New Jersey, New York, Pennsylvania, Rhode Island, or Vermont
South Atlantic...504	Delaware, District of Columbia, Florida, Georgia, Maryland, North Carolina, South Carolina, Virginia, or West Virginia

Notes

___

Chapter 1: The Missing Data: Spiritugraphics

1. *Mad Men*, season one, episode eight, "The Hobo Code,"directed by Phil Abraham, written by Chris Provenzano, aired September 6, 2007, emphasis added.
2. Besheer Mohamed, "New Estimates Show U.S. Muslim Population Continues to Grow," Pew Research Center, January 3, 2018, https://www.pewresearch.org/fact-tank/2018/01/03/new-estimates-show-u-s-muslim-population-continues-to-grow/.
3. Dr. David Naugle, Worldview: Definitions, History, and Importance of a Concept (Dallas: Dallas Baptist University, n.d.), 1, https://www3.dbu.edu/naugle/pdf/Worldview_defhistconceptlect.pdf.
4. Francis A. Schaeffer, *How Then Shall We Live?: The Rise and Decline of Western Thought and Culture* (Wheaton, IL: Crossway, 2005).

Chapter 2: Forerunners and Benefactors

5. David Ogilvy, *Ogilvy on Advertising* (New York: Random House, 1983), 9.
6. QSR Staff, "These 29 Fast-Food Brands Earn the Most Per Restaurant," *QSR Magazine*, August 2020, https://www.qsrmagazine.com/content/these-29-fast-food-brands-earn-most-restaurant.
7. QSR Staff, "These 29 Fast-Food Brands Earn the Most Per Restaurant."
8. QSR Staff, "These 29 Fast-Food Brands Earn the Most Per Restaurant."
9. Ogilvy, *Ogilvy on Advertising*, 15.
10. "Who We Are," Chick-fil-A, accessed March 18, 2022, https://www.chick-fil-a.com/about/who-we-are.
11. *Mad Men*, season one, episode six, "Bablyon,"directed by Andrew Bernstein, written by Andre and Maria Jacquemetton, aired August 23, 2007.
12. Snopes Staff, "Do In-N-Out Burger Food Containers Include Bible Verses," Snopes, December 7, 2002, https://www.snopes.com/fact-check/in-n-out/.

13 Michelle Gant, "Why Does In-N-Out Print Bible Verses on Its Cups and Wrappers?" *TODAY,* October 9, 2019, https://www.today.com/food/why-does-n-out-print-bible-verses-its-cups-wrappers-t164235.

14 "Glassdoor Reveals Employees' Choice Awards for the Top CEOs in 2019," Glassdoor, June 18, 2019, https://www.glassdoor.com/about-us/top-ceos-in-2019/.

15 Brian Solomon, "Meet David Green: Hobby Lobby's Biblical Billionare," *Forbes,* August 18, 2012, https://www.forbes.com/sites/briansolomon/2012/09/18/david-green-the-biblical-billionaire-backing-the-evangelical-movement/.

16 James Aldridge, "Hobby Lobby Increasing the Minimum Pay for Hourly Store Employees," *San Antonio Business Journal,* updated March 20, 2013, https://www.bizjournals.com/sanantonio/news/2012/04/16/hobby-lobby-increasing-the-minimum-pay.html.

17 "Hobby Lobby Raises Minimum Wage," Hobby Lobby Newsroom, September 14, 2020, https://newsroom.hobbylobby.com/articles/hobby-lobby-raises-minimum-wage/.

18 "Hobby Lobby Raises Minimum Wage," Hobby Lobby Newsroom.

19 Kelly Tyko, "Hobby Lobby Raises Minimum Wage to $18.50 an Hour for Full-Time Workers Starting Jan. 1," *USA Today,* updated December 15, 2021, https://www.usatoday.com/story/money/shopping/2021/12/14/hobby-lobby-minimum-wage-increase/8897355002/.

20 Tyko, "Hobby Lobby Raises Minimum Wage."

21 Solomon, "Meet David Green."

22 Cheryl Sloane Wray, "Family and Business: A Winning Combination for Hobby Lobby's David Green," Birmingham Christian Family, June 28, 2021, https://birminghamchristian.com/family-and-business-a-winning-combination-for-hobby-lobbys-david-green/.

23 Jerry Bowyer, "Restoring Trust Through Trusts: Hobby Lobby CEO Is a Steward, Not an Owner," *Forbes,* May 1, 2017, https://www.forbes.com/sites/jerrybowyer/2017/05/01/restoring-trust-through-trusts-hobby-lobby-ceo-is-a-steward-not-an-owner/.

24 Bowyer, "Restoring Trust Through Trusts."

25 Irene Anna Kim, "How Toms Went from $625 Million Company to Being Taken Over by Its Creditors," *Business Insider,* updated December 27, 2020, https://www.businessinsider.com/rise-and-fall-of-toms-shoes-blake-mycoskie-bain-capital-2020-3.

26 Irene Anna Kim, "How Toms Went from a $625 Million Company to Being Taken Over by Its Creditors," *Insider,* December 27, 2020, https://www.

businessinsider.com/rise-and-fall-of-toms-shoes-blake-mycoskie-bain-capital-2020-3#:~:text=Toms%20grew%20quickly%2C%20thanks%20to,canvas%20shoe%20and%20giving%20model.

27 Blake Mycoskie, "A Conversation," Fresh Life Church, January 6, 2019, https://subsplash.com/freshlifechurch/messages/mi/+dh8nv6q.

28 Associated Press, "Blake Mycoskie on 10 Years of Toms," Business of Fashion, May 6, 2016, https://www.businessoffashion.com/articles/news-analysis/blake-mycoskie-on-10-years-of-toms/.

29 Patrick Range McDonald, "Is Blake Mycoskie of Toms an Evangelical," *LA Weekly*, July 28, 2011, https://www.laweekly.com/is-blake-mycoskie-of-toms-an-evangelical/.

30 Meg Cichon, "Help Them Help You: IKEA to Donate Solar Lighting to Refugees with Each LED Bulb Purchase," Renewable Energy World, February 10, 2014, https://www.renewableenergyworld.com/baseload/help-them-help-you-ikea-to-donate-solar-lighting-to-refugees-with-each-led-bulb-purchase/#gref.

31 "Dive Right In! The Journey of McDonald's Filet-O-Fish," McDonald's, accessed March 18, 2022, https://corporate.mcdonalds.com/corpmcd/en-us/our-stories/article/ourstories.filet_o_fish_journey.html.

32 "5 Popular Holidays for Flower-Giving in the U.S.," Fresh Trimmings, January 28, 2019, https://bouqs.com/blog/holidays-for-flower-giving/.

33 Harry J. Enten, "Christmas May Be on the Cards, But Is It the Most Popular American Holiday?," *The Guardian*, December 22, 2012, https://www.theguardian.com/lifeandstyle/us-news-blog/2012/dec/22/christmas-cards-holidays-us.

Chapter 3: Americans and Faith

34 PRRI Staff, "The 2020 Census of American Religion," PRRI, July 8, 2021, https://www.prri.org/research/2020-census-of-american-religion/.

35 PRRI Staff, "The 2020 Census of American Religion."

36 PRRI Staff, "The 2020 Census of American Religion."

37 Barry A. Kosmin and Ariela Keysar, "American Religious Identification Survey," Trinity College, March 2009, http://commons.trincoll.edu/aris/files/2011/08/ARIS_Report_2008.pdf.

38 PRRI Staff, "The 2020 Census of American Religion."

39 "Religious Landscape Study," Pew Research Center, accessed March 18, 2022, https://www.pewforum.org/religious-landscape-study/.

40 PRRI Staff, "The 2020 Census of American Religion."

41 PRRI Staff, "The 2020 Census of American Religion."

42 PRRI Staff, "The 2020 Census of American Religion."

43 PRRI Staff, "The 2020 Census of American Religion."

44 PRRI Staff, "The 2020 Census of American Religion."

45 Kosmin and Keysar, "American Religious Identification Survey."

46 "Religious Landscape Study," Pew Research Center.

47 "Religious Landscape Study," Pew Research Center.

48 Krystle M. Davis, "20 Facts and Figures to Know When Marketing to Women," *Forbes*, May 13, 2019, https://www.forbes.com/sites/forbescontentmarketing/2019/05/13/20-facts-and-figures-to-know-when-marketing-to-women/.

49 "Statistics on the Purchasing Power of Women," Girlpower Marketing, accessed March 18, 2022, https://girlpowermarketing.com/statistics-purchasing-power-women/.

50 "Buying Power (Quick Take)," Catalyst, April 27, 2020, https://www.catalyst.org/research/buying-power/.

51 "Religious Landscape Study," Pew Research Center.

52 "Religious Landscape Study," Pew Research Center.

53 "Religious Landscape Study," Pew Research Center.

54 "Religious Landscape Study," Pew Research Center.

55 "Religious Landscape Study," Pew Research Center.

56 PRRI Staff, "The 2020 Census of American Religion."

57 PRRI Staff, "The 2020 Census of American Religion."

58 PRRI Staff, "The 2020 Census of American Religion."

59 PRRI Staff, "The 2020 Census of American Religion."

60 PRRI Staff, "The 2020 Census of American Religion."

61 PRRI Staff, "The 2020 Census of American Religion."

62 PRRI Staff, "The 2020 Census of American Religion."

63 PRRI Staff, "The 2020 Census of American Religion."

64 PRRI Staff, "The 2020 Census of American Religion."

65 PRRI Staff, "The 2020 Census of American Religion."

66 PRRI Staff, "The 2020 Census of American Religion."

67 PRRI Staff, "The 2020 Census of American Religion."

68 PRRI Staff, "The 2020 Census of American Religion."

69 PRRI Staff, "The 2020 Census of American Religion."

70 Claritas Data, JDA Worldwide, https://claritas.com/data/.

71 Jeffrey M. Jones, "U.S. Church Membership Falls Below Majority for First Time," Gallup, March 29, 2021, https://news.gallup.com/poll/341963/church-membership-falls-below-majority-first-time.aspx.

72 Lydia Saad, "U.S. Satisfaction Sinks with Many Aspects of Public Life,"

Gallup, February 4, 2021, https://news.gallup.com/poll/329279/satisfaction-sinks-aspects-public-life.aspx.

73 Frank Newport, "More U.S. Protestants Have No Specific Denominational Identity," Gallup, July 18, 2017, https://news.gallup.com/poll/214208/protestants-no-specific-denominational-identity.aspx.

74 Kosmin and Keysar, "American Religious Identification Survey."

75 Kosmin and Keysar, "American Religious Identification Survey."

76 "Religion," Gallup, accessed March 18, 2022, https://news.gallup.com/poll/1690/religion.aspx.

77 Jones, "U.S. Church Membership Falls Below Majority for First Time."

78 Saad, "U.S. Satisfaction Sinks with Many Aspects of Public Life."

79 Gabe Rosenberg, "Study: 91 Percent of Women Feel Misunderstood by Advertisers," Contently, July 1, 2014, https://contently.com/2014/07/01/study-91-percent-of-women-feel-misunderstood-by-advertisers/.

Chapter 4: America's Research Group National Behavioral Study

80 "Barbara Kruger's I Shop Therefore I Am—What You Should Know," Public Delivery, January 28, 2022, https://publicdelivery.org/barbara-kruger-i-shop/.

Chapter 10: Spiritugraphic #5: Small Town Ideals

81 John Mellencamp, *Scarecrow*. Riva, 1985.

Chapter 11: Spiritugraphic #6: Lent

82 'The Future Needs More Workers," Carhartt, accessed March 19, 2022, https://www.carhartt.com/build-a-better-world.

Chapter 12: Spiritugraphic #7: Not-So-New Media

83 Chip Gaines and Joanna Gaines, "Our Story," Magnolia Network, accessed March 19, 2022, https://magnolia.com/about/.

Chapter 14: Spiritugraphic #9: Daughters Are Different

84 "Our Heritage: Birth of an Icon," Ivory, accessed March 19, 2022, https://ivory.com/our-heritage/

Chapter 15: Spiritugraphic #10: Not Yet Woke

85 R. Albert Mohler, *The Gathering Storm: Secularism, Culture, and the Church* (Nashville: Thomas Nelson, 2021).

Acknowledgments

——

L ike most new business frameworks, the Spiritugraphics work has been informed over many years and by many people. We're specifically grateful for the remarkable people who have made brilliant contributions to our industry through their work at JDA Worldwide. To them, it's more than a vocation; it's been a labor of impact. The hundreds of teammates whom we've had the privilege to work alongside have influenced this book mightily, with nuanced insights derived from a life spent serving our clients well.

Additionally, we'd like to recognize the major role that our exceptional clients have played over the past two decades, daily providing challenges and opportunities to think differently for our team that have led to these understandings. We thank our friends, whom most would call clients, who trust us with their most difficult objectives and have been true partners toward a better world.